THE STUDENT'S GUIDE TO PHILOSOPHY

THE STUDENT'S GUIDE
TO PHILOSOPHY

Peter A. Facione
California State University, Fullerton

Mayfield Publishing Company
Mountain View, California

A.M.D.G

Library of Congress Cataloging-in-Publication Data

Facione, Peter A.
    The student's guide to philosophy.

    Includes index.
    1. Philosophy—Introductions.   I. Title.
BD21.F33   1987   100   87-24864
ISBN 0-87484-832-6

Manufactured in the United States of America
10 9 8 7 6 5 4 3 2 1

Mayfield Publishing Company
1240 Villa Street
Mountain View, California 94041

Sponsoring editor James Bull; production editor, Linda Toy;
manuscript editor, L. Jay Stewart; text and cover designer,
Andrew H. Ogus; cover photograph by Peter Southwick/Stock
Boston. The text was set in 10/12 Goudy Old Style by Kachina
Typesetting and printed on 50# Finch Opaque by Malloy
Lithographing, Inc.

CONTENTS

Knowledge

Logic

Nature

Religion

Theory

PREFACE

To the Student

Over the past twenty years of teaching, I have come to know and appreciate the difficulties you face when you first encounter the discipline of philosophy, particularly if that first experience occurs in a required course outside your major. So I wrote this study guide for you. It is designed to help you:

- gain an overview of philosophy and philosophical thinking
- keep basic philosophical concepts and arguments straight
- progress quickly to a more complete and sophisticated understanding of philosophical issues
- improve your own philosophical thinking skills
- and, as a result, do a better job on exams and assignments

But don't assume you must read this book from the front to the back! Actually the best way to use this study guide is to skip around. Because the sections are largely self-contained, you can focus on those that connect with your own needs. You may want to select sections that parallel the reading assignments or lecture topics in the course you are taking. If you are more knowledgeable, you might use particular sections to review once-familiar territory.

To get the most out of this book, take the initiative and read actively. At first, spend a moment trying to answer the opening question at the start of a section. As you read the rest of the section, pause to entertain objections to arguments. Try to anticipate replies to these objections and the implications of distinctions, definitions, and theories. Think through the questions for further inquiry at the end of each section. Then question how your initial perspective on a given issue has been challenged, strengthened, refined, expanded, or changed?

Through this study guide, I am hoping to share the wonders and challenges I have found and enjoyed in philosophy with you. Each section is a crisp, no-frills sketch of a basic position, concept, problem, or theory. But philosophy is as much a process of thinking as it is a collection of issues and perspectives. Because of this, I used two different text formats. At times you will see a narrative format that outlines key concepts clearly and concisely. More often, I use a pro-and-con discussion format, that is designed to illustrate philosophical thinking and engage you directly in this vital process. As debates unfold, you can practice your own philosophical skills by anticipating responses. And you will also experience how to make intellectual progress through grappling with key conceptual issues philosophically.

To My Colleagues

This study guide is intended for introductory, general education courses in philosophy or as background in selected topics courses. It is designed to supplement, not substitute for, such valuable pedagogical resources as primary source readings, discussion articles, case studies, films, guest speakers, and class lectures and discussions. This guide is intended to assure broad coverage of fundamental issues, stimulate student thinking, and create the flexibility needed to organize class time in interesting and fruitful ways.

Peter A. Facione

THE STUDENT'S GUIDE TO PHILOSOPHY

PHILOSOPHY

P-1   QUESTIONS AND CONCERNS

Question: What, in general terms, is philosophy about?

Procedure: When you first encounter a new subject or concept, try to get a broad, general understanding first. Then, after that, refine your idea by adding more and more precision. Finally, as you master the details, use this knowledge to go back and sharpen your original general understanding.

Definitions and Characterizations

Philosophy, throughout its varied and complex twenty-five-hundred-year history, remains a reasoned inquiry in pursuit of wisdom regarding the most fundamental questions that affect the human condition. In general terms philosophy can be defined or understood as:

* the love of wisdom, from the Greek meanings of *philo* and *sophia*
* a disciplined inquiry into the principles that underlie ethical conduct, human thought, and the nature of the universe
* the persistent effort to think things through carefully
* a disciplined reflection on life's fundamental questions
* a comprehensive world view based on a consistent set of assumptions about human nature, ethical conduct, and the methods of achieving truth
* the speculative probing of the limits of the possible and the knowable

1

Traditional Philosophical Concerns

Value theory examines the theoretical basis for making decisions regarding values and inquiries into whether those decisions can or cannot be justified. Value theory includes: *ethics,* which focuses on discovering the basic principles upon which we should base our judgments about the moral rightness or wrongness of behavior; *aesthetics,* which is concerned with values relating to beauty and how they are determined or ascribed; *social and political philosophy,* which explores the value implications of the social structures and political institutions within which individuals and groups of people interact; and *metaethics* (meaning beyond ethics), which is concerned with the ultimate nature of values—how to understand the meaning of value statements and how to make correct inferences regarding values.

Theory of knowledge, known as *epistemology,* inquires into the sources, nature, and limits of human knowledge. Among the questions raised are the reliability and veracity of sense perceptions and the relationship of human knowledge to belief, doubt, faith, mystical revelations, and so on.

Metaphysics inquires into the most fundamental or basic nature of reality, the existence of a deity, human nature, human freedom, personal identity, consciousness, minds, time, space, the soul, and like concerns.

Logic, including critical thinking, inquires into methods and patterns of inference and, in particular, into ways of accurately assessing the logical strength of arguments and uncovering fallacious reasoning.

Metastudies, or the *philosophy of* _____, inquires into the basic assumptions, broad theoretical issues, and methodological processes of a given discipline, for example, the philosophy of science, the philosophy of education, the philosophy of mathematics, or the philosophy of history.

Applied philosophy studies specific questions within various areas of human endeavor, research, or concern. Examples include the philosophy of law, business ethics, medical ethics, the philosophy of death and dying, or environmental ethics. Applied philosophy can also be focused on more specific issues such as the nature and meaning of "machine learning."

The history of philosophy—although not strictly a philosophical inquiry, but an historical one—supplies background information essential to the practice of philosophy. The historian of philosophy seeks to interpret, analyze, and expand our knowledge about specific philosophers or philosophical traditions, such as the Greek philosophers, Socrates or Plato; the influence of Thomas Aquinas; the development of Aristotle's principles of logic in the Middle Ages; the contrasts between Hume and Kant on key issues in epistemology; the impact of Marxist thought on political and religious thinkers in contemporary South America; the implications of Wittgenstein's philosophy for machine-based language processing and translation; the evolution of existentialist thought in the decades since World War II; the impact of the analytical and phenomenological traditions on American pragmatism.

The Rule of Reason

Over the past twenty five hundred years, a diverse number of philosophical traditions have flourished at various times. Many include, and are even defined in terms of, their own specific "method" of philosophical inquiry. No single official method of philosophy exists. There are, however, some important limitations and guidelines within philosophical inquiry. One is that philosophers must *demonstrate* what they claim to be the case, basing their *arguments* on logical reasoning and true premises. (See P-4 and L-3.) In philosophical disputes, one should debate logically and base her or his reasoning on statements known to be true.

Areas for Further Inquiry

Consider the following claims:

• At certain moments people step back from the din of daily life and confront, with an attitude of curiosity and wonder, the complexities of the universe and the uncertainties of life.

• At such times questions come to mind regarding reality. These questions seem to be fundamental and enduring in character, such as, What is the meaning of life? How can I be certain? Does God exist? Are my choices really free? What is the right thing to do? In the final analysis, what is reality? Is there life after death?

• The wise person is one who knows the answers to all such questions, and moreover, the wise person's answers are not self-contradictory.

• Beyond what I immediately perceive happening to me right at this moment, nothing can be known about anything unless I make certain assumptions, for example, that I am not now experiencing illusions, that I can trust my memory of things past, that some things are good and others are bad.

• Once we have found the most reasonable and reliable assumptions, we can build an integrated world view based on our own experiences and solid reasoning. We can then trace the implications of what we believe and thus seek to expand both our knowledge and our wisdom.

Is each claim above true exactly as it stands, or would you want to add clarifications and suggest exceptions? For example, does wisdom really imply knowing answers to every question? Must we make assumptions in order to know something? If so, what kinds of assumptions?

If you were to list the "fundamental and enduring" questions, would your list be the same as those suggested above? Do questions like those even make sense? If they do, how might a person go about answering them?

What is the relationship of philosophy to scientific investigation and to religious revelation? Can a given statement be true and false at the same time (e.g., true religiously speaking, but not in terms of science)?

P-2   AIMS AND PURPOSES

Question: What is the goal of philosophical inquiry?

Strategic consideration: One way to discover a person's goals is to examine not what the person says, but what the person does. The wonder, reflection, and careful inquiry that characterize philosophical thought must be guided by some set of purposes, aims, or goals toward which philosophers strive. By looking at what philosophers do, we may gain an understanding of what their goals are.

First Observation

•   Philosophers challenge people to explain the meanings of things that at first seem perfectly easy to understand. For example, What is justice, beauty, right, truth, freedom, reality, illusion?

•   Philosophers question whether concepts are properly applied. For example, Can we really call this a case of free choice, or was the person socially conditioned to act this way?

•   Philosophers try to clarify the meanings of words by describing the boundaries of concepts with careful definitions. For example, the concept of God includes the properties of being all-powerful, all-knowing, and all-good—indeed perfection. When we ask, then, if God exists, we are not talking about a limited deity, but rather the existence of the most perfect being conceivable.

•   Philosophers try to eliminate vagueness and ambiguity to the extent that the subject matter allows. For example, let's distinguish between "science" as the product of empirical inquiry and "science" as the process of conducting such an inquiry. Or, another example, the term *critical thinking* is too vague to be helpful unless we limit our discussion to "reasoning advanced in support of a conclusion, which reasoning is expressed publicly in the form of statements in a written or spoken language."

Given the above, it appears that *one goal or aim of philosophy is to critically analyze ideas and thereby achieve precision and clarity of thought and expression.* (Sections such as E-6, G-1, G-2, F-5, F-6, K-1, N-6, N-8, and R-1, among others, pursue this purpose.)

Second Observation

•   Philosophers try to discover the connections between concepts and the implications of these concepts. For example, if having rights derives from one's capacity for rational thought rather than from a metaphysical principle such as possessing a soul, then some species of higher animals must also be said to have rights.

• Philosophers seek to articulate fundamental, general concepts and theories that are broadly applicable. For example, the purpose of this essay is to show that the scientific theory of evolution is consistent with a faithful, but nonliteral, interpretation of Scriptural creation accounts.

• Philosophers develop alternative models and analogies that help explain, confirm, and extend the applicability of key concepts. As an example, a more fruitful way of thinking about the relation of the individual to society is to see each person as a cell in a living organism rather than as an interchangeable part in a lifeless machine.

So philosophy not only tears ideas apart, but it also builds them up. Thus *another goal or aim of philosophy is to achieve comprehensive, systematic understanding.* (Sections such as those on freedom, knowledge, nature, religion, and theory, among others, emphasize this goal.)

Third Observation

• Philosophers demand that people give reasons to justify their beliefs. They are constantly asking, Why? or What's your reason for thinking that?

• In philosophy everything is open to question, including all our beliefs, the arguments for them, and the assumptions upon which those arguments are based. For example, if you can't give a basis for your opinion, then you have no right to hold that opinion. Believing things without good reasons is irrational behavior.

• Philosophers insist on carefully reasoned arguments. For instance, from what has been said so far, we can infer only that time travel toward the future is a logical possibility. But, notice, we have not yet established the same regarding time travel toward the past.

• At another level, philosophers attempt to evaluate the adequacy of competing theories, analogies, models, concepts, kinds of arguments, or systems of thinking. Philosophers advance *metalevel* theories in order to codify and explain how such evaluations should be conducted. For example, using Aristotle's theory of syllogisms, this kind of argument would be valid; however, using contemporary logic as developed by Bertrand Russell, it can be shown that the argument's supposed validity rests on a crucial, and possibly false, assumption that generalizations must be about nonempty classes.

These concerns suggest that a *third goal or aim of philosophy is to expand the role of reason in human affairs.* (Section P-4 and those on logic and metaethics, among others, focus on this goal.)

5

Fourth Observation

• Other academic disciplines and fields of investigation limit their study to finding out what *is* the case. By contrast, philosophers throughout history have asked, What *ought to be* the case?

• Philosophers consider a variety of value-related issues. They ask how value judgments are made, how they are justified, and what they signify. For example, in ethics one might ask, If a conflict arises between my duty to respect human life and the survival of an entire city, would I not be justified in sacrificing a few people for the sake of thousands? Or, in another example, if I am sure I know what is right for the nation, am I not justified in breaking the law to achieve it?

• After considering value questions such as these, philosophers often make recommendations regarding the morally correct course of action, or they advance theories that can serve to guide one in deciding on the correct course of action. For example, when faced with a moral decision, always act so as to respect the value of yourself and all the other persons involved.

Thus, *philosophy's fourth aim or goal is to guide evaluation.* (The sections in ethics and government, among others, emphasize this goal.)

Areas for Further Inquiry

• Given that philosophy, in general, aims at being analytically precise, systematically comprehensive, carefully reasoned, and evaluative, does it follow that a person is not a philosopher unless he or she pursues all four goals? Or does it mean that everyone who pursues all four goals is necessarily a philosopher? To prove your point, give a specific example or counterexample.

• The goals of analytical precision and careful reasoning suggest a conservative effort to avoid error and accept only those ideas that we can know with certainty to be true. By contrast, the goals of comprehensive systematicity and value inquiry suggest bold, imaginative efforts to extend knowledge to its limits and maximize the possibility of believing the truth even if our grounds for belief are insecure. When these two thrusts come into conflict, as they surely must, which takes priority—minimizing the risk of believing what is false or maximizing the possibility of believing what is true?

• Is the initial, guiding strategic assumption above—namely that one can discover a person's goals by examining their behavior—right? What counterexamples can you construct? What qualifications, if any, would you put on that idea? Remember what you experience with the proposal leading off this section because other initially plausible suggestions or ideas you will encounter in this text (or in your life) may also seem good at first, yet they might require revision and qualification after you have carefully explored them.

P-3   MAKING PROGRESS

Question: If the questions philosophy concerns itself with are enduring, in what sense is any progress ever made?

Challenge: If solving problems and moving on to new issues constitute progress, then philosophy, for all its twenty-five-hundred-year history, has not made much progress!

The Case for Thinking Philosophy Makes No Progress

In general there are two ways for a systematic study to make progress: Either (a) it finds solutions to problems, or (b) it advances to the consideration of new questions. By contrast, a quick review of the history of philosophy suggests that philosophers throughout the centuries have been concerned with the same general range of problems, such as, What is the moral life and how can I achieve it? Is there a God and, if so, how do I relate to the deity? What is the ultimate nature of reality? Can I know anything for certain? What am I as a human being? Do I have a free will? Am I purely a physical thing? And, Does life have meaning?

As for solutions to these problems, those offered by any one philosopher seem to be refuted and rejected by others. You can always find a philosopher who disagrees and apparently with good reason. So the questions never seem to be really settled, and the agenda never seems to advance. For these reasons, it follows that the discipline of philosophy makes no intellectual progress.

Three Responses to the Argument That Philosophy Makes No Progress

First: Individual Progress in Achieving Wisdom Is Possible.   Given the way it defines "making progress," the argument above presumes that the goal of any disciplined study, such as philosophy, is the piling up or accumulation of knowledge. But philosophy seeks *wisdom*, not a mere collection of facts or solutions to puzzles. Wisdom does not imply an increase in information, but rather an increase in understanding. To be a seeker of wisdom involves learning to value clear insights, healthy perspectives, balanced judgments. Wisdom involves not just thinking wisely but acting wisely as well. Achieving wisdom is an individual thing. It is possible through philosophical reflection to achieve greater wisdom. In this sense, individuals can indeed make philosophical progress.

Second: Collective Progress from Generation to Generation Is Possible. Philosophical questions endure because they are *important and fundamental to appreciating and understanding the human condition.* Whereas the questions endure, the people and the times change. Each new generation must rethink these questions for their own time and place in human history. In grappling with the enduring and fundamental questions of life, each new generation makes its own progress.

Learning how earlier generations have reflected on the same questions and also seeing the objections registered to the "solutions" of earlier times, we can gain insights into various ways of thinking about the human condition, and we can avoid the mistakes of the past. Thus we make progress in the sophistication, articulation, elaboration, and refinement of our philosophical perspectives. In this sense, progress in philosophy can be a collective cultural achievement as well as an individual one.

Third: Progress Includes Perfecting One's Intellectual Skills. A person practices an instrument not just to hear a melody, but to refine her ability as a musician. Similarly, one practices the discipline of philosophy to perfect one's intellectual tools. Philosophical reflection can lead to greater skill in thinking critically, in finding more comprehensive connections between concepts, in being more precise in the expression of one's ideas, and in being more adept at making reasoned value judgments. Thus progress—understood not as sets of answers, but as the refinement of intellectual skills—can be achieved through the study of philosophy.

Areas for Further Inquiry

• Considering what philosophy is, as described in P-1 and P-2, wouldn't it be reasonable to expect that progress in solving specific problems is indeed a legitimate goal of philosophy? If so, then doesn't the original case against philosophy stand despite the three responses above?

• The third response, which sees the value of philosophical reflection as a means to improving one's thinking, confuses the goal of making progress in the resolution of philosophical questions with a possible side benefit of studying philosophy. But a distinction exists between a *goal* and a *result.* Thus might we agree that philosophy is beneficial to study but still maintain that it will never lead to new knowledge. If this is so, then no real progress is possible. This, however, raises another question: How many kinds of "progress" or ways of "making progress" are there?

• The entire discussion regarding progress assumes that progress is good, that it is always worthy of desire. But is it? Under what conditions and to whom might philosophical progress be harmful?

- Socrates (469–399 B.C.) said that wisdom begins with the realization of ignorance. If he was right, then what should one's first steps be if one is interested in becoming wise?

P-4   GIVING REASONS

Question: It is essential in philosophy to give reasons in support of your position, but how can a person evaluate the quality of someone's reasoning?

Insight: Even if we cannot look inside a person's head, we can decide whether to accept the claims a person makes by looking at the arguments the person offers on behalf of those claims.

Basic Strategy

Think of the claim a person is making as the conclusion in an argument and the reason the person offers in support of the claim as the premises of that argument. Why think in this way? Because the conclusion and the premises of an argument can be expressed in language as statements. (For example, everyone is mortal. So Socrates is mortal.) As a result, *an argument reveals a person's reasoning* in language, thus opening it up to analysis and evaluation. Reasons might be private, but arguments are public. They are open. We can hear them, read them, think about them, evaluate them, reject or accept them.

The strategy of converting a person's reason into a set of premises and a person's claim into a conclusion has this benefit: The question of evaluating how well a person's reason supports his or her claim becomes the more objective questions of whether a given set of premises is true and whether it logically implies or justifies a given conclusion.

Key Definitions

An *argument* is a *set of statements*, one of which, the *conclusion*, is the claim that the author of the argument is trying to demonstrate or prove to be true; the other statement(s) are the *premise*(s) that the author of the argument offers as a reason to accept the conclusion.

For example: If the President was aware, then he should have told the press everything. If he was not aware, then he should have fired his aide. Either he was aware or not. Therefore, the President should have fired his aide or else told the press everything. (Here the conclusion is the final sentence.)

For example: Very few AIDS victims survive more than sixty weeks from the onset of symptoms. This is what statistical surveys done in 1985 and 1987 in California and New York suggest. (Here the conclusion is the *first* sentence, as often happens.)

A person often has more than one reason for believing a given claim, and so the person may offer more than one argument. Think of each reason as a new and independent *set of premises*. Separate reasons yield separate arguments, each of which must be evaluated in turn.

For example: Another reason, beside the survey data, why most AIDS victims don't survive more than sixty weeks is that once the symptoms of the disease are evident, the disease has progressed so far that the person is less and less able to fight infections, and our health care establishment has no way of helping the person.

Presumptions of Rational Argumentation

When honest people are engaged in a sincere effort to discuss an issue of mutual concern, they presume certain things in their conversation. For one, they presume when offering statements on behalf of their claims that these statements are more or less obviously true to the other person. That is, they don't intentionally use erroneous information or lie to each other. If a disagreement about the truth of any statement arises, then each party makes a reasonable effort to check out the facts, or the person qualifies the force with which he wishes to assert and maintain his conclusions.

A second thing people presume is that their claims follow from or are dependent upon their reasons. That is, the premises they use explain why their claim should be considered true. By contrast, the truth of the premises is presumed *not* to depend on the truth of the claims a person is trying to establish. Truth runs from premises to conclusion, not the other way. If challenged, an individual's defense of any given premise would be to argue for that premise by appealing to more basic beliefs and assumptions, not by appealing to the presumed truth of the ultimate conclusion.

Evaluating Arguments

There are three steps in deciding whether a person's argument ought to be accepted as a demonstration of the truth of its conclusion.

First: Find the Argument

Identify the claim or conclusion the author of the argument intended to establish. Identify the premises the author explicitly presents on behalf of that conclusion. Identify any unstated assumptions the author intends to be taken as additional premises. In this step critical reading or careful listening are the keys.

Second: Rewrite the Argument

Restate the author's argument using all and only those statements the author intended to serve as either premises or the
conclusion. In this step careful interpretation and attention to
accuracy, honesty, and fairness are important.

Third: Assess for Logical Strength and Truthfulness

The purpose of arguments then is to preserve and transmit
truth from premises to a conclusion. Arguments that fail, for
whatever reason, in this truth-preserving role are bad arguments. One way to assess the logical strength and truthfulness
of an argument is to use *both* of the following tests:

The first test: Try to imagine a situation in which *all the premises of the
argument are true, yet its conclusion is false.* How likely, given all you know about
the subject at hand, is that situation to occur? If it is *impossible* or *extremely
unlikely,* then the argument is logically strong. But if you can think of an *actual
or possible* situation in which all the premises are true at the same time that the
conclusion is false, then to the extent that such a situation is real or might
happen, the argument is logically weak. The more real the situation is or might
be, the weaker the argument.

The second test: Are all the premises in the carefully and fairly reconstructed
version of the argument actually true? Since a good argument is one that
(speaking metaphorically) transmits the truth of its premises into its conclusion,
even if the transmission is well done, unless all the premises are true, you cannot
rely on the conclusion to be true. Notice also that if the premises are not
consistent with each other, that is, if they contradict each other, then they
cannot *all be true at the same time.* Thus, this test really asks that an argument's
premises be judged as a group, not individually. If the premises taken together
are true, this test is passed.

> If a person presents an argument in accord with the pre-
> sumptions of rational argumentation, and the argument passes
> *both* tests, then you should accept the argument as a good
> demonstration of the truth of the author's claim.

Areas for Further Inquiry

• Isn't there a more reliable way of testing an argument's logical strength than
leaving it up to the powers of a person's imagination? Yes, there is. Much
contemporary work in logic and statistical research methodology is aimed at
trying to find more reliable ways of handling just this issue. (See "Logic.")
Obviously, handling the second test—for the truthfulness of the premises—can

11

also be a problem. Carrying this test off depends on the extent of a person's background knowledge, hence the value of a solid liberal education.

•   What if the conclusion of an argument is true by definition and the premises of the argument also happen to be true yet have no relevance to the conclusion? In such a case, the argument would pass the two tests, but we would not want to accept it as a *demonstration* of its conclusion. How could we rule out such arguments? Should we invent a third test, perhaps one measuring the relevance of the premises to the conclusion? Assuming it is possible to test for relevance, what objective criteria might such a test employ?

ETHICS

E-1   EGOISM

Question: Should self-interest be the guiding principle of conduct?
Contention: People always do what they want to do. Any ethical theory that ignores this ignores human nature.

An Argument for Ethical Egoism

Ethical egoism, like other theories in ethics, is a theory about how people *ought* to behave. Theories about how we ought to behave are called *normative* theories because they express value judgments about what *should* or *ought* to happen. *Ethical egoism* specifically is the view that people should always act so as to maximize their own personal welfare or self-interest.

An advocate of *ethical egoism* might begin by observing that people *do* act as if motivated by self-interest; indeed, that self-interest is the *only* motive upon which people can act. Since ethical positions should be based on what people actually do, acting out of one's own self-interest is the wise and morally proper thing to do.

Ethical Egoism and Selfishness

A critic of this viewpoint might naturally object saying, "Ethical egoism as a normative theory embodies dreadful value judgments. It encourages selfishness and the immediate gratification of one's lowest, animal desires. To live as an ethical egoist would make a person truly obnoxious. And it would be foolish, too. After all, some things a person wants are self-destructive. It just isn't wise to always do whatever you please."

"You're missing a vital point," the ethical egoist could reply. "Self-interest need not be unenlightened. A thoughtful person can, with foresight, discover her or his self-interest in more subtle and refined ways of acting, including practicing such virtues as self-control and temperance. One's *enlightened* self-interest may also include building friendships and achieving self-respect. Obviously it isn't wise to do whatever you please, nor is it in your self-interest. Acting on the basis of enlightened self-interest does not imply gratifying self-destructive desires."

"But," the critic might respond, "how can an ethical egoist morally engage in cooperation with others or do any self-sacrificing work? How could such a person ever be a good coworker, a good friend, or a good parent?"

"Relax," the ethical egoist would say to this. "Both cooperation and self-sacrificing labor fit with the idea of enlightened self-interest so long as your principal goal in doing these things is to *benefit yourself.*"

Ethical Egoism and Psychological Reality

"Wait a minute," the critic might interject, "you can't make cooperation depend on the motive of self-interest. The truth is people do not always act with the goal of benefiting themselves. Sometimes yes, but not always. Self-sacrificing self-interest doesn't even make sense."

"I agree," the ethical egoist could reply. "It doesn't. So let's not pretend that people sometimes act with a view toward serving the interests of others. It is a psychological fact that they don't. They can't."

"I don't agree. What about altruistic motives? What about sacrificing your own life for your children or your friends?"

"Take a closer look at those cases," the ethical egoist might point out. "You will find that apparent cases of self-sacrifice or altruistic motivation are really done out of self-interest. A person cannot help but act out of self-interest; doing otherwise is a psychological impossibility. The origins of society are from primitive tribes of people acting out of self-interest. Children act out of self-interest. So, both socially and individually, we find our roots in self-interested action."

The critic might continue to object. "No. Your argument doesn't hold. First, it incorrectly assumes that in primitive tribes people act out of self-interest. But anthropologists often speak of primitive tribal organization as being more communally oriented, with greater importance given to working for the welfare of the total community than to serving one's own self-interest. Another problem with your argument is that it falsely assumes that no transformations are possible, no growth can occur, no relevant differences can exist between primitive stages of individual or social development and more mature stages. Just as societies can change, so can individuals. Human nature is not fixed, unchanging from birth to maturity. A person's range of motivations and interests expands

14

with maturity and can come to include acting with the idea of benefiting others as a principal goal."

The ethical egoist, however, might rejoin, "Cases of apparent motivations beyond self-interest are simply cases of self-deception or cases where the person is really motivated by self-interest, but the person is not conscious of the effects of that motivation."

Exploration. The ethical egoist is asserting the view that humans act on the basis of self-interest exclusively and universally. This view is called *psychological egoism*. It is a theory about the motivations with which humans *do* act, rather than a theory about how humans *ought* to act. Since this is a theory about actual human motivation, it comes under the realm of scientific inquiry. As such, is this theory true? What experimental basis is there to support this theory? Do you agree with resorting to talk of "unconscious motivations" and "self-deception" as ways to respond to counterexamples of apparently non-self-interested behavior? What evidence might the psychological egoist accept as counting against this theory? If none, then can the theory really be considered scientific or experimental?

Do the Facts Decide the Issue?

"So what," the ethical egoist might say. "Even if psychological egoism is false—which it isn't—the normative theory, ethical egoism, is correct. Self-interest *should* be the chief principle upon which people decide what is right and wrong."

"That's backwards," the critic might object. "Even if psychological egoism were true—which it isn't—that people *do* act only out of self-interest does not imply that people *ought* to act that way. Normative claims about what *ought to be* cannot be inferred from claims about what *is*. Besides, you're confused. If there's a scientific basis to believe that people always act out of self-interest, then the argument that we *ought* to behave that way doesn't make sense. We cannot *not* behave that way. *Ought* implies *can*, but according to you, in this case we cannot!"

"I'm not confused," the egoist might assert. "Granted we cannot help acting out of self-interest, but there's still great value in consciously accepting the normative principle of enlightened self-interest. Our entire economic theory is based on the hypothesis that individuals act from enlightened self-interest. So, as people become more enlightened in their pursuit of self-interest, everyone will benefit because the economy will work the way it's supposed to. Also, by consciously accepting the normative principle of self-interest, people will be better able to resist being misled by other normative theories that are wrong."

Exploration. What is the inferential relationship between what *is* the case and what *ought* to be the case? Value judgments do not occur in a factual vacuum, but in what sense and to what degree are facts relevant to making value judgments? To draw a conclusion about what *ought* to be, must we always start with at least one premise that expresses a value judgment? What is the relationship between *ought* and *can*? Does *ought* imply *can*, even though *can* does not imply *ought*?

If the ethical egoist is mistaken, should contemporary Western economic theory be radically revised?

Philosophical Role Playing

As an ethical egoist, how would you reply to the following?

• To act on the basis of my own interests is not the same as acting on the motivation of self-interest. My interests as a mature adult are broader than my own welfare. I am interested in helping others and in caring for my children, family, friends, and community. It makes me happy to do these things, but that is not why I do them—don't confuse a result with a goal. I don't give Christmas gifts to make *me* happy; nor is it *in my interest* to give away my property, yet I am very happy when I see how much others enjoy my gifts. If I accepted ethical egoism, then it would be *immoral* for me to give gifts since right now my chief motivation in giving them is to benefit others, not myself.

• Moreover, self-interest stops at death, but my interests and motivations can extend beyond my own death. People give their lives and their labor to do things to benefit art, knowledge, country, future generations, the environment, their church, world peace, and so on. They find that doing these things which make a significant contribution to things beyond themselves and their own short existence on this earth make life meaningful. Not only does this count as evidence against the psychological theory of egoism, it is also an objection to the normative theory. For if we accept ethical egoism, then people *ought not* do such things as these. As a result, life for many would be less meaningful.

E-2   SOCIAL UTILITY

Question: How can people reach objective agreement on ethical matters?

Proposal: Actions that result in the greatest good for the greatest number of people are better than other actions.

An Argument for Utilitarianism

Consequentialist normative theories propose that an action's moral value is determined by looking at the results it produces. One important consequentialist theory is *utilitarianism*. In its classical form, utilitarianism maintains that we ought always to act so as to promote the greatest good for the greatest number of people.

An advocate of *utilitarianism* might begin by observing that some states of affairs are simply better than others. Since people can often foresee the states of affairs their actions bring about, they can also foresee the relative value of various alternative courses of action. To this a classical utilitarian, such as John Stuart Mill (1806–1873), would add the normative judgment that it is always better to promote the greatest possible net amount of good over bad. Also, the more people who benefit as a result of an action, the better that particular action is compared to its alternatives. It follows, then, that people ought to act so as always to promote the greatest good for the greatest number.

What Is Better Than What?

Utilitarians must make it clear how to distinguish objectively which states of affairs are better than others. Utilitarians consider certain states of human consciousness to have *intrinsic* value (that is, value in themselves). Specifically, pleasure and happiness are good, whereas pain and unhappiness are bad. But since pleasure and happiness are not the same, the question arises, which of these is better? And, in general, the question persists, what should we do if people disagree over which states of consciousness have greater value? To this question utilitarians might reply, "Our theory does not *require* any assumptions about human nature or about which states of consciousness are better than others. Whereas some might maintain that certain pleasures are higher or of greater intrinsic quality than others, strictly speaking our emphasis is on individual autonomy in stating one's preferences. Each of us has the freedom to decide the states of consciousness that are better for us."

Exploration.   An initial goal of classical utilitarianism was to provide an objective basis to rationally resolve disputes over value questions, such as disputes over public policy. How does the response in quotes above square with that goal?

Quantifying Value

In speaking about the "greatest amount of good," utilitarianism assumes that moral values can be meaningfully quantified and measured. This might be done the same way objective value judgments are made in commerce, industry, and many other areas of human endeavor—by establishing agreed-upon standards and clearly applicable procedures of measurement. Granting that the actual consequences of any course of action are highly difficult to predict, utilitarians propose that we measure the *potential, relative moral value of alternative courses of action* based on our *best estimate of the foreseeable consequences* produced by each alternative.

A utilitarian response might advocate, when measuring the quality of various states of affairs, considering four factors: (1) *intensity,* or how strongly or weakly the good or bad consequences will be felt, (2) *duration,* or how long the

17

good or bad experiences will last, (3) *propinquity*, or how near or far in the future the consequences are, (4) *extent*, or the number of persons involved or affected. When comparing the relative merits of alternative courses of action, consider three more things: (5) *purity*, or the likelihood of producing the greatest net amount of good over bad results, (6) *fecundity*, or the tendency of immediate consequences to keep other options open and, thus, contribute to greater amounts of desirable consequences later on, and (7) *certainty*, or the probability that the predicted consequences will occur.

Exploration. Does it work? Are the standards plausible; are they applicable? How, for example, do you calculate intensity or certainty? If you are having trouble, consider this reply: "Yes, it is difficult to compare one person's grief with another's joy. But one does the best one can under the circumstances. These kinds of calculations are, indeed, hard to make. But that does not mean we should not try to make them!" Is this kind of reply adequate?

What if, contrary to one's estimates, the actual consequences of an action turn out bad when we had foreseen good? Is one responsible for what *actually* happened or for only what *was foreseen?* Utilitarians seem forced by the logic of their theory to respond that, objectively speaking, *a person did wrong if the actual consequences turn out badly.* They can soften this by adding that the amount of blame a person must suffer can be reduced to the extent that the person made an honest effort to forecast accurately. But, like the coach with a losing season or the general who lost the war, too bad! Do you agree?

Whose Happiness?

The critic of utilitarianism might inquire, "Why is it better to benefit more people rather than fewer? What if I wished to consider only the benefits to myself or to some limited group of people, such as just the people living in my home state or belonging to my private club?"

The utilitarian could reply, "There is no moral basis for preferring the interests of one person or subgroup over those of another. Thus, until a morally compelling reason emerges, the presumption must be that everyone's interests, including one's own, count equally."

"Perhaps that's true," the critic might agree. "But that only delays the question. What counts as a 'morally compelling reason'? Do gender or racial differences count? On strict utilitarian grounds, there is no way to prevent people from making unfair discriminations."

Exploration. Some believe that utilitarianism can work only when other baseline values, such as *respect for all persons* (see E-3) and *justice* (see G-1 through G-3), are already in place. Given your current understandings, do you think that an appeal to other values such as respect for all persons can be justified on strictly utilitarian grounds?

The Good of Each and the Good of All

"What happens to the common good?" the critic might remark. "That's easy," the utilitarian could reply, "the common good is simply the net of positive over negative results for each individual in a community."

Exploration. The utilitarian's reply assumes an atomistic, rather than organic, model of human communities. But good coaches and successful managers know that for a team or group to enjoy success, they cannot simply let each member pursue his or her own individual goals. How much are communities like teams? Can you imagine a case in which the good of each person in a community works against the common good? If each person is responsible for her or his own interests, who is responsible for everyone's?

Specific Actions or Rules of Behavior

The critic might observe, "Some actions, such as lying, generally lead to bad consequences, but at times a lie can lead to good results. Should I lie in those cases but not generally? Or wouldn't I be justified in assassinating a Hitler type to save the world from a major war?"

Utilitarians are of two minds regarding how to reply to this line of inquiry. Those who advocate what is called *act utilitarianism* would say, "Yes, because each action is to be evaluated separately by its own consequences." Those who advocate *rule utilitarianism*, however, would say, "No, actions are to be considered in terms of general practices. And as general practices, lying and political assassination have been found to yield more bad than good results." Which approach seems wiser to you: evaluating actions individually or in light of tried and true general rules of conduct?

Philosophical Role Playing

As a utilitarian, how would you reply to the following:

• In calculating the greatest good for the greatest number, should we consider the interests of potential persons? For example, in developing policy on the use of natural resources, should we consider only those people alive today, or must we also consider future generations? If both, do people living today and future generations count equally? Should a person's potential children be counted as equal to one's present children?

• Animals as well as humans can experience pain. Why consider only human states of consciousness as having value? If animal pain has negative value, how do we quantify it in comparison to human pain?

• One useful way to calculate value is in terms of dollars. As a matter of social policy, how much is one person's life worth?

19

E‑3   CATEGORICAL IMPERATIVES

Question: Regardless of consequences, are not some actions morally right and others morally wrong?

Contention: The morality of an individual's action is determined not by how successful the action is in achieving some result but by the ethical character of the action considered in itself.

An Argument That People Have Unconditional Moral Duties

Some claim that we should not look at the consequences of our actions to judge if the actions are right or wrong; rather we should look at the ethical quality of the actions themselves. An advocate of this view might begin by asserting, "Some actions, like killing innocent people, enslaving people, lying, breaking promises, deliberately ignoring responsibilities, indiscriminately consuming resources, or cheating are unconditionally wrong. Further, the very same action cannot be right for one person and unconditionally wrong for another person. Indeed, as a general rule, if something is morally wrong for one person to do, then it would also be wrong for all others. So it follows that our moral obligation is to conduct ourselves in accord with our unconditional moral duties and to refrain from all actions that are morally wrong."

Initial Questions

A critic might challenge, "First, what about the duties that arise as a result of social convention or because we plan to accomplish a worthy goal? Are these also our unconditional moral duties? Second, where did your list of right and wrong actions come from? How do you know which actions are morally right or wrong in themselves?"

Hypothetical and Categorical Duties

As good philosophers often do, the advocate of this view will make the theory more sophisticated by introducing certain important conceptual distinctions and guiding principles in response to the critic's questions. "First, those duties that arise out of social or legal conventions (e.g., my contractual duty to pay my rent) or as a result of some purpose or goal we hope to achieve (e.g., my duty to study in order to earn my degree) can be regarded as *hypothetical imperatives*. They become duties because they are instrumental in achieving some further result. *If* I desire that result, then I have a given duty. However, morality—strictly speaking—is concerned not about hypothetical imperatives but about *categorical imperatives*. Categorical imperatives are those that constitute our *unconditional* ethical duties for they apply in all possible circumstances regardless of our goals or the results of our actions."

To the second question—Where does the list of categorical duties come from?—there are many possible answers. Historically people have said that to discover one's duty one must attend to the dictates of conscience or look at divine revelation or follow one's moral intuitions or live by the values of one's cultural tradition. What do you think about these four replies? Could you defend any of them from the criticisms that they lack objectivity, are underdirective, or depend on questionable assumptions?

Another approach leads to discovering categorical duties. The German philosopher Immanuel Kant (1724–1804) formulated three alternative expressions of the categorical imperative. These are crucial for students of philosophy and can be restated as:

• Act so that your decision could serve as a principle of universal law applying to similar actions of similar agents in circumstances similar to yours.

• Act so as to treat everyone, including yourself, always as an end possessing intrinsic value and never as a means only.

• Make your decisions about your own actions as if you were a legislator participating in establishing the laws for an imaginary kingdom (moral community) of persons considered as ends in themselves.

The Principle of Universalizability

The critic might object, "But there are ethically relevant differences between people—such as abilities, levels of knowledge, maturity, social circumstances—that make an action wrong for one person but not for another. For example, it is wrong for me to sleep with your spouse, but not for you. How does your theory handle this observation?"

"Not by denying it," the advocate would answer. "Ethically relevant differences in terms of the agent and the circumstances of the action do exist. The formulation of the *principle of universalizability* (the first formulation above) takes these into account better than my original argument did."

"Yes, but I can apply the principle of universalizability to things that seem trivial. For example, everyone should brush their teeth before going to bed. I can also apply it to practices that seem immoral and also conflict with other formulations of the categorical imperative. For example, always treat the shortest member of a group of ten men as the slave of the other nine. This principle doesn't supply enough information to define my duty."

"By itself it is not sufficient to completely express your duty," the advocate would have to agree. "But universalizability is still a necessary condition for determining moral duty. That means, *anything that violates the principle of universalizability is certainly immoral.*"

To this, the critic—partially vindicated—would also agree.

21

Good Intentions

"Some things are wrong, and I'll avoid doing them," maintains the critic, trying to lay a trap. "Now tell me. Does that mean I'm being an ethical person? For example, suppose I obey the speed limit because if I don't I may get a traffic ticket."

How would you answer?

In response to the critic, the advocate—not wanting to connect the ethical value of any action with how good or bad its consequences might be—would say, "To determine the rightness or wrongness of an action look at your *intention*. If you acted out of a desire to achieve or avoid potential consequences, you were *not* acting morally. But if you acted with the intention of doing your duty, regardless of the consequences, then you were acting morally."

Challenges to the Categorical Imperative

Shifting his focus to the three formulations of the categorical imperative, the critic makes three objections. "To begin with, the second formulation seems too strong. It suggests that I can't even ask someone to do me a favor for I would be treating the person as a means to serve my needs. Second, even with all three formulations in hand, my specific duties are still vague. For example, I know I should not interfere with your efforts to get a good education, but am I obligated to help you pay for it? Does my obligation to speak the truth mean that I must inform the government about the crimes of my fellow citizens or must I tell people things that I know will only hurt their feelings? Third, the three formulations are inconsistent because I can easily imagine cases where every choice I might make is immoral. Say, for example, that a murderer demands to know where I hid my friend, but I promised my friend I would never reveal the hiding place. But suppose the gunman asks if I know where the hiding place is. Either I must lie to the gunman or break my promise. Both are immoral under this theory of ethics. But what kind of theory is this if, in cases like this, every choice is unethical?"

The advocate of this theory might offer the critic the following clarifications. "First, you didn't read the second formulation carefully enough. It says you cannot treat yourself or others as a means *only*. That is, you cannot manipulate people or treat them as tools or things. But people can still freely agree to help each other. Second, regarding knowing exactly how far your duties extend, we agree on the minimum (noninterference) even if we are still vague about how far your maximum responsibility extends. Finally, your example is faulty. There *is* a third choice; you could keep silent."

Philosophical Role Playing

As an advocate of the view that some actions are ethically right or wrong in themselves, how would you have replied to the three questions just raised by the critic in regard to the categorical imperative? How can we flesh this theory out to respond effectively to the vagueness issue? Or can't we? And what if the critic comes up with a slightly better example. How are we going to respond to the challenge that in certain circumstances inconsistent moral demands are made?

The concept behind the three formulations is that people are inherently and intrinsically valuable (have value in themselves). So, we should always treat people—including ourselves—with profound respect as ends in themselves and members of the same moral community. What specific duties does respecting one's self and others entail?

Duty and respect for persons can conflict with self-interest (E-1) or social utility (E-2). For example, being honest on your income tax return could conflict with self-interest, or spreading untruths by "cover-ups" and "disinformation tactics" may have great social utility. Although you may not have yet looked at sections M-1 through M-4, still—in your opinion—what is the ethical thing to do when different values or ethical duties conflict?

E-4   RIGHTS AND DUTIES

Question: What are my moral rights and obligations as a person?

Proposition: To judge which actions are morally good or bad, one must take into consideration one's natural and conventional rights and duties.

An Argument That Morality Is Based on Rights

Consider the following argument: "As a person I have certain moral rights that are natural, independent of government or social convention, for example, the right to life and personal liberty. Also, as a social being, I have rights that arise out of the conventions of society and law, for example, the right to make contracts, to select my own friends and companions, to trial by jury, of freedom of assembly, to a decent job, to a free basic education, to emergency medical treatment, and other similar rights. As a general rule, the rights of one person imply the duty of all others not to interfere with the exercise of those rights. Also, rights are precisely the kinds of things that may not be superseded nor surrendered. So when I am exercising my rights, I'm behaving ethically; and when I interfere with the rights of others, I'm morally wrong."

Identifying Moral Rights

The critic, impatient to begin the assault, starts off. "You make it sound so simple and obvious. First, even if I were to agree that there are *natural* or *basic* or *fundamental human rights*, how we can identify precisely what these are is far from clear. For example, are control over one's own body, death with dignity, control of the rearing of one's own children, freedom of speech, freedom

23

of thought, and freedom of religion—just to name a few things—basic or natural human rights?

"Second, I'm not sure your concept of *conventional rights* is much better. Each person may be a member of several communities at one time, such as a family, neighborhood, educational or occupational community, social club or organization, and so on. The conventions governing one's roles in these communities define one's *prerogatives* (rights) and *obligations* (duties) relative to each community. However, *conventional expectations* (what you expect you are entitled to do and what others expect you are obligated to do) *are not always clear, consistent, or unchanging.* For example, regarding *clarity*, consider 'free basic education.' Does that mean entirely without cost; does it include basic preprofessional education at the postsecondary level; does it include midlife career retraining? Regarding *consistency*, consider how your occupational duties can conflict with your family or possibly your religious obligations. Regarding *changeability*, think about how your legal rights and duties can be altered by legislative changes, for example new tax laws that change your deductions or increase your taxes."

The advocate of a rights theory of ethics might reply, "Discovery of one's *natural* rights and correlative duties is difficult but not impossible. One might begin with the concept of respecting all persons as intrinsically valuable in themselves. This implies treating yourself and others as equal members of the moral community—as ends, not just means. (See E-3, "Categorical Imperatives.") And, yes, one's *conventional* rights are complex and relative to the expectations of one's roles in a given set of communities. I agree, conventional rights are not necessarily clear, consistent, and unchanging. But complexity, in itself, is not an objection."

Exploration. Does connecting *natural* moral rights with respect for persons solve the problem? Would it also help to connect *natural* moral rights with concepts like *justice* (see G-1) and *autonomy* (see F-5)? Because "natural" suggests that some rights come from God, natural law, or a metaphysical analysis of human nature, some philosophers believe a more neutral adjective, such as "nonconventional," should be found. Do you agree?

Correlative Duties

The critic might reply, "Complexity is a problem! Because of the complexity of *conventional* rights, it is not clear that all rights imply the duty of noninterference. For example, I have the conventional right to start a business, but you have the right to start a competing business. You have *the right*, in other words, *to interfere!*"

"You have a good point," the advocate might remark. "So, to clarify, let's say the *correlative duty of noninterference* is connected with *all natural* rights. That is, no individual may interfere with another's proper exercise of a *natural* right. Some, but not all, *conventional* rights imply that other individuals have the *correlative* duty of noninterference."

Exploration. The complexity of conventional rights seems to extend the concept of *correlative duties* beyond simply noninterference. For example, the duty to pay taxes comes about in part because of the government's goal of redistributing wealth and assisting disadvantaged persons in achieving equal social and economic opportunities. "Free" education, to name just one example, is not without its costs. However, it is the duty of other, more able, members of society to bear those costs. By contrast to the conservative list of rights that might have been advanced in the eighteenth century, today many of the rights people assert are correlated with *duties on the part of others to take positive steps* to assure that those rights can be exercised. To what extent should people individually or as a group be responsible for making it possible for others to exercise their rights to decent medical treatment, equal employment opportunity, free use of the highways, a college education, a competent legal defense, safe and dignified employment, or a secure retirement?

Superseding and Surrendering Rights

The critic might press further, "Initially you said that rights were the kinds of things that could neither be superseded nor surrendered. This doesn't fit with the facts. Rights of both kinds, natural and conventional, can be superseded either partially or entirely. As an illustration, a criminal's natural right to life and liberty may be overridden to protect the rest of society. The conventional right to make a profit is limited by legal and moral requirements regarding fraud, extortion, and fair competition. Also, rights of both kinds may be voluntarily surrendered. One may decide to surrender one's natural right to rear one's own child by permitting the child to be adopted. One may surrender one's conventional right to control of one's property by making contributions to charity."

A right that may not be overridden under any circumstances is called *indefeasible.* The violation of such a right, whether by another individual or the state (government) is never justified. The Bill of Rights in the U.S. Constitution lists some natural rights considered to be indefeasible. By being included in the Constitution, these natural rights are also protected as *conventional legal rights.*

A right that may not be given away is called *inalienable.* The American Declaration of Independence lists some natural rights considered to be inalienable. Question: How did those who wrote this important historical document know which rights to put in the list?

Areas for Further Inquiry

• How might the advocate of the theory that our ethics are defined in terms of rights and correlative duties respond to the observations that both kinds of rights, natural and conventional, can be superseded and surrendered?

• In moral terms, are the rights and duties of individuals and governments the same? Do governments have the right to interfere with an individual's rights even if other individuals may not? Do governments have any natural rights, for example, the right to strive for continued existence?

E-5   THE LIFE OF VIRTUE

Question: How can I achieve "the good life"?

Reconsideration: Instead of evaluating discrete actions, ethics should focus on evaluating patterns of actions with special attention to enhancing one's capability to realize intrinsic value.

Focus on a Person's Character, Not Actions

Some philosophers think that the kinds of theories discussed in earlier sections are all flawed because they focus only on the ethical evaluation of individual actions. They believe ethics should be concerned with the totality of a person's life, not discrete behaviors and decisions.

Advocates of this view might argue, "One's life should form a meaningful, integrated whole. Living well means weaving a tapestry that creatively integrates the various threads of one's human capacity into a beautiful, fulfilling, and self-actualizing style or pattern of life. The realization of a great number of human potentials is intrinsically good, for example, health, pleasure, knowledge, aesthetic creativity, appreciation of art, autonomous functioning, decision making, achievement in a specific area of endeavor, friendship, and living with others in peace and harmony. So, the ethical focus should be on the cultivation of certain character traits (virtues) that will lead to living well, that is to *the good life.*"

Defining "The Good Life"

Critics of this view scoff at the phrase "the good life," saying, "It means too many different things to different people. Are these philosophers naively suggesting there is *only one* correct interpretation or meaning of the good life? If so, does it mean happiness, wisdom, pleasure, power, or what?"

Such ambiguity leads to a second objection. The idea of living the good life seems shallow and self-centered. Maybe "good-life" theories, or "virtue" theories as they are sometimes called, are just disguised versions of ethical egoism. (See E-1.)

Exploration. Given that many candidates exist for what constitutes the good life, how would you propose to decide which is superior? You need not exclude the more noble ideals either. There is nothing necessarily selfish or self-centered about good-life theories. Devoting one's energies to civic affairs, education, health care, or public service can all be important elements of a person's concept of living a fulfilling, meaningful life. Whereas Aristotle (384–322 B.C.) and other classical theorists of the life of virtue emphasized the values of civic responsibility, contemporary culture seems disenchanted with the ideal of a life devoted to service or society. Certain contemporary subcultures seem entirely oriented toward personal gratification. In view of these ambiguities and inconsistencies, can good-life theories overcome the charge that they are not really "ethical" theories at all?

Virtues

The objection that good-life theories are not necessarily theories of ethics can be reinforced by noticing that not all virtues are ethically desirable. By definition, *virtues* are character traits that contribute to a specific goal. Thus, the military virtues are not the same as the artistic virtues. Virtues are inner motivators. They represent the disciplined tendency of persons to decide to act in ways that are consistent with and conducive to a given goal without recourse to external positive or negative sanctions. But a character trait that is a virtue relative to one goal could be a vice (liability) relative to another. For example, always telling the truth might reduce used car sales! Also a specific virtue might not be morally *good*. For example, physically intimidating opponents is an athletic or military virtue that many would regard as an ethically undesirable characteristic.

In response to this kind of objection, advocates of the *good life theory of ethics* might introduce a key distinction. They could point out the difference between the *material* level and the *formal* level. The focus of virtue theories could be at either level, of course. For example, at the material level, a given philosopher might advocate a certain list of virtues as morally superior to others: honesty, purity, truthfulness, cooperativeness, thoughtfulness, loyalty, bravery, cleanliness, self-reliance, modesty, thrift, and so forth.

However, advocates of the good life theory of ethics often maintain that discussions regarding the specific content of the good life, and hence the specific character traits to cultivate, are best left up to each individual. Thus, if you want to be a warrior, cultivate courage and physical strength, or if you want to be a scholar, cultivate intellectual curiosity and learn how to do research. But, unless asked for personal advice, advocates of the good life theory of ethics find it unproductive to dwell too long with concerns at the material level.

The Formal Virtue of Integrity

The good life theory of ethics thus does not presume any single definition of "the good life" at the material level, that is, at the level of potentials a person actually selects to try maximizing. By contrast, it does take a stand at what is called the *formal* level. There is a central virtue at this level, the *formal virtue of integrity*. Integrity, from the verb "to integrate," refers to the capacity of a person to integrate decisions and actions with his or her interests and capabilities meaningfully and thoughtfully, given the limitations and potentialities of life. In this sense integrity means living a life of balance and internal harmony. (Notice that the word *integrity* as used here does not mean the same as the word *honesty*.)

In response to the question, Is integrity the only virtue? advocates of this view often identify several other character traits that are conducive to achieving "the good life," *using any definition of intrinsic goals at the material level*. The other formal virtues are:

• knowing and appreciating the finitude of human life and how finitude impacts on efforts to lead an integrated life;

• accurately assessing and accepting one's own abilities and limitations;

• being moderate in one's desires and deeds because of an awareness of the dangers associated with extremes of behavior or desire;

• accepting authority and accountability for making decisions and commitments affecting one's self and others, within the limits of what can be known and achieved;

• persevering with one's efforts to achieve a life of integrity given the uncertainty, adversity, and limitations of one's existence;

• endeavoring to achieve one's full potential and to overcome the limitations and uncertainties one faces in life.

Philosophical Role Playing

As an advocate of the good life theory of ethics, how would you respond to the following statement: Our lives are limited by our social circumstances, the viewpoint-oriented nature of individual awareness, the concreteness of our existence, the stage of our development as human individuals, and the knowledge that we are finite entities. Thus no one can achieve full potential. Moreover, trying to maximize *all* of one's potentials to achieve intrinsic good can be intensely frustrating if not self-defeating. It would take a superhuman to maximize every physical, intellectual, artistic, and social potential she or he is blessed with. The ideal of living a meaningful life can never be achieved.

E-6   MEANING OF LIFE

Question: Does human existence have ultimate meaning?

Definition: An event can be considered significant or meaningful if it is valuable in itself or brings about something valuable in itself.

The Concept of a Meaningful Life

The concept of finding life meaningful came up several times in the earlier ethical discussions. The question, Does human life have ultimate meaning? requires a careful analysis of the concepts involved.

We might begin by considering this point of view: Life can be considered to be an event or series of events. And one's life can be meaningfully spent if the events in that life are conducted in an effort to achieve goals that are valuable in themselves. Or, alternatively, one's life can be called meaningful if the pattern of events in that life is in itself valuable. If every event in life can be meaningful, life as a whole can be meaningful. So, either as a means to a noble goal or as an end in itself, a person's life can be ultimately valuable and meaningful.

Critics of this argument could point out a number of problems. For one, it seems illogical to say that what is true of the parts must also be true of the whole. It is possible that the individual events should seem meaningful, but that the life as a totality be pointlessly absurd.

Critics might also point out that a fundamental ambiguity resides in the expression "human life." Are we talking about one person's life, part of one person's life, a series of people's lives (e.g., myself, my ancestors, and my offspring), the life of humans as a biological species, or all life on earth? Then, too, what does *meaningful* mean? Are we limiting the discussion to goal-oriented behavior or the pattern of behavior, or are we saying that *meaningful* implies that life is an omen or sign pointing beyond itself—such as to some ultimate divine plan for the universe?

Clarifying the Question

To cut through the critic's objections, let's focus on whether one person's life, taken as a totality, can be meaningful. If one life is meaningful, then each person's life can be meaningful. If that is so, then human life as a whole can be meaningful. Let's also agree that saying a life is meaningful means either that it has been devoted to a noble and worthy purpose, or it has been lived so coherently as to be valuable in and of itself.

To these proposals, the critic might still object, "No, we must separate arguments regarding the meaningfulness of each person's life from those regarding the meaningfulness of human life taken as a whole."

"But," we might reply, "this is not a matter of cold logic. A complex relationship exists between an individual's finding his or her own life meaningful and the way in which that individual relates to others. The meaningfulness of a single life in isolation may not even be possible. If it can be shown that even one life is meaningful, then we have both the logical possibility and the emotional hope of finding other persons' lives, including our own, meaningful."

Exploration. Would our reply be adequate? What is the relationship of the individual to the totality of other humans as a community, a state, or a species? How might the meaningfulness of one person's life be influenced by the meaningfulness of someone else's life or of human life as a whole?

The critic might voice other objections to our proposals. "First, if a person is only pursuing self-interest or defining his own values, then those values will have no depth. Even if they were important *to that person,* what reason is there to suppose that others would share those values or find it meaningful to live their lives in accord with them? And, in the final analysis, how could it be known that the values an individual has chosen are the right ones? Second, if we rely on God to define ultimate value, doesn't that introduce all the problems of whether God exists and how we are to know what God values?" (See R-1 through R-7.)

We might reply, "First, consensus on the list of things valuable in themselves is not essential. Some might include love, glory, self-respect, happiness, wisdom, health, or the flourishing of one's self, one's community, or one's children. So long as a person is willing to commit to something, that person's life has the potential of being meaningful. Second, for the religious person, God is the source of all that is valuable and meaningful. Through salvation, God removes the obstacles preventing people from living meaningful lives. God infuses human lives with purpose and shows how best to live. Thus, God makes our lives, individually and collectively, meaningful."

Exploration. What if, however, a person is not religious? What other responses might be made to the second objection? Is religious faith essential for human life to have an ultimate meaning? Finding meaning in life seems to depend on knowing what is valuable in itself. How can we know what is valuable? Who decides? Who invests something with intrinsic value—the individual, tradition, the government, God, public opinion, the family? What if, as Jean-Paul Sartre (1905–1980) and others maintain, life is, in the final analysis, absurd?

Slips Along the Way

The critic might argue, "Things can go wrong. Purposes may fail to be achieved, effort may turn out to be futile or frustrated. If that happens, does life fail to have meaning? In retrospect, was it all for nothing? Patterns of behavior can also be upset, people can make inconsistent decisions, incoherence can enter the picture. In these cases, does life fail to have meaning?"

Exploration. Would this reply be adequate: "Even if the noble goal wasn't achieved, so long as the person did not spend her life doing things she knew would not achieve the goal, the person's life would be meaningful. So long as the person doesn't intentionally act incoherently or inconsistently, the person's life is meaningful."

If a person lives a life dedicated to some supposedly worthy goal, but in the end learns that the goal could never have been achieved or was really all a sham, how does that affect the evaluation of the person's life as meaningful or absurd? Does it make sense to say that a person's life was partially meaningful or that only part of it was meaningful?

Areas for Further Inquiry

Is suicide ever rational? If so, does it invalidate the possible meaningfulness of that person's life? In what sense does your response regarding suicide apply to the same question regarding self-sacrifice? How are self-sacrifice and suicide different from a moral perspective?

Is there a difference between the question, Does human life have meaning? and the question, Does human life have *ultimate* meaning? If so, how might the answer to one affect the answer to the other?

METAETHICS

M-1 RESOLVING VALUE CONFLICTS

Question: How can value conflicts be resolved rationally?
Thesis: Setting priorities, finding alternatives, and compromise are strategies for easing normative tensions.

Tensions Involving Values

Three distinct situations might be described as value conflicts.

1. A given value might conflict with itself. For example, faced with several obligations, one wonders which to honor.

2. The value conflict might be between persons. For example, seeking justice, one wonders how to be fair in distributing benefits and burdens to the different members of a group.

3. One value might conflict with another value. For example, duty might conflict with self-interest, or social utility might conflict with equity.

This third situation is the paradigm case we must address. But first we should distinguish three different kinds of value tension that can arise.

1. *Divergence:* a situation in which one choice seems more desirable for one set of reasons whereas another choice seems more desirable for another set of reasons. The two choices, however, are not mutually exclusive.

2. *Simple conflict:* a situation in which accepting a given set of circum-stances, or a given selection of means to a specific goal, would lead one to select between mutually exclusive alternatives.

3. *Essential conflict:* an unavoidable situation in which acting on one alternative will imply the inevitable impossibility of acting on another. For example, deciding to play a professional sport would force one to forego participating as an amateur athlete in the next Olympic Games. Essential conflict usually arises over *goals*, whereas simple conflict is usually a matter of *means* or *circumstances*.

Strategies for Resolving Value Tensions

After one has clarified which values are at stake, one might explore the possibility of using one or more of these three strategies in attempt-ing to resolve the normative tensions.

1. *Set priorities:* Determine which values, goals, persons, consequences, and so on are more important than others. Decide if any are so important that you consider achieving them essential. Decide which are more fundamental; that is, safeguarding them is a precondition for achieving anything else. Decide which are more encompassing; that is, accomplishing them yields the broadest range or highest level of achievement.

2. *Be flexible:* Dissolve simple conflicts and divergent tensions by finding alternatives such as doing both, doing neither, changing the problematic circumstances, selecting a different means to a given goal.

3. *Seek compromises:* When setting priorities seems irrational and no alternatives can dissolve the tensions, try to identify values that might be partially, rather than fully, realized.

Areas for Further Inquiry

• Setting priorities presumes finding a rational and objective criterion for deciding one thing is more important than another. For example, is justice more important than peace? Is social harmony more important than an individual's right to life? Under what circumstances would setting priorities *not* be a rational or feasible strategy?

• Being flexible implies creativity, innovation, and prudent planning. But people cannot control everything, and they cannot foresee every consequence or every alternative. Also, adversity is desirable at times. It builds character and leads to strength of purpose. How important is it to maintain one's options as compared to achieving certain intrinsically valuable goals that are best approached by surrendering some or all of one's flexibility? (For example, marriage, choosing a mayor, selecting a career goal, deciding where to live, having children.)

•   Rational compromise is possible only if values can be partially realized. But certain values cannot, or should not, be compromised. Also, striving for compromises presumes that all parties to a dispute have some right to be included in the negotiated settlement. To compromise with criminals or because one is forced to negotiate by someone more powerful hardly makes compromise entirely noble or justified. Compromise your moral principles, sounds like strange advice. Should we exclude this strategy from the list?

M-2   NORMATIVE STATEMENTS AND ETHICAL RELATIVISM

Question: How should assertions expressing values be interpreted?
Definition: A statement that expresses a value judgment is called a normative statement.

The Domain of Ethics and Value Theory

Ethics is the field of philosophy that focuses on discovering the basic principles upon which people *should* judge the moral rights or wrongs of human behavior. As such, ethics is concerned with normative statements, particularly those that have immediate implications for individual human behavior. In contrast to the urgings of prudence or etiquette, ethical concerns are thought to be more serious for either of two reasons: They involve the potential for significant harm or benefit for oneself or others, and they express conformity or violation of the dictates of duty, respect for persons, or the rights of persons. Ethics deals both with *goals* and with *means* to those goals. Ethics is also highly concerned with the justifications given for normative claims.

Ethics includes theoretical and practical concerns. It is a disciplined, normative study that tries to resolve practical, moral problems with rational argumentation. Ethics also questions the adequacy of more general ethical principles and the universal moral standards people rely on in specific situations.

Ethics focuses on (1) questions of intrinsic and absolute value, (2) objectivist interpretations of those questions, and (3) providing reasons in support of the wisdom or superiority of certain normative claims over other normative claims. Let's clarify this by defining our terms.

The Basic Concept of a Normative Statement

Normative statements are assertions that express value judgments. Some normative statements have immediate behavioral implications. For example, "You should ask someone to drive you home now." In this respect, normative statements are similar to imperative sentences. By contrast, other statements, called *nonnormative*, are value neutral. They are not intended to express value judgments; often these are reports, descriptions, assertions of fact, even opinion (so long as they avoid expressing a value judgment).

Normative statements resemble nonnormative statements in four ways that make the application of rational argumentation plausible.

1. People do in fact offer reasons, from time to time, on behalf of their normative assertions.

2. People evaluate the adequacy of the reasons others offer regarding normative assertions.

3. People recognize that certain combinations of normative statements form inconsistent sets of beliefs.

4. People derive entailments from normative statements. Thus we can reasonably ask why people think a given normative statement is "true" or at least why it is "wise," "justified," or "reasonable."

Important Distinctions

Objectivist Versus Subjectivist Interpretation.   The *objectivist* interpretation treats normative statements such as "X is right," as claims that there is *something about* X which makes it worthy of being preferred independently of the speaker's actual personal preferences. By contrast, the *subjectivist* interpretation of the same statement treats it as a claim *about the speaker,* namely that that speaker desires or prefers X.

Intrinsic Versus Instrumental Values.   Things that are considered to be valuable in and of themselves are called *intrinsically* valuable, for example, happiness, intelligence, virtue, life, pleasure, liberty, social harmony, honor, integrity, friendship. (Or to list common negative intrinsic values: pain, ignorance, boredom, terror, frustration, loneliness, discord.) Things that are desired as means to achieving something else are called *instrumentally* valuable. Examples include money, creativity, knowledge, skill, opportunity. (Certain negative instrumental values are poverty, ignorance, weakness, lack of time, lack of cooperation, incompetence, distractions, mistrust.) Some things, such as health, peace, and wisdom are often considered to be both intrinsically and instrumentally valuable.

Absolute Versus Relative Values.   When something is instrumentally valuable because of social convention, it can be called a *relative* value. For example, not smoking in a restaurant, keeping one's lawn trimmed, avoiding crude and vulgar language, starting and ending events at the scheduled times, and so on are relative values. They contribute instrumentally to public health, sustained property values, respect for other persons, and the smooth flow of commerce. When something is worthy of value independently of the mores or conventions of any given society, it can be considered an *absolute* value. Public safety, respect for life and property, peace, love, prosperity, and the like might be candidates for consideration as absolute values. But then, again, maybe no values are absolute!

Justification Versus Excuse. To attempt to *justify* an action is to claim the action was the right thing to have done. "It was my duty to protect the president. That's why I pushed him to the pavement. And, I would do it again if I thought he was in a similar danger." By contrast, to give an *excuse* for an action is to admit the action was wrong and to ask to be held not fully accountable for the action. "Yes, I did push the president to the pavement, but it was an accident. I tripped and stumbled into him. I meant him no harm, and I apologize."

Areas for Further Inquiry

• The analysis of normative statements above suggests that they show important similarities to nonnormative statements with regards to being used in rational argumentation. But many normative statements are considered neither true nor false. How much does this weaken the claim that they can be used as the premise or conclusion of an argument?

• Some things may turn out to be common to all or most intelligent societies, such as providing for the survival and continuation of the community, helping individuals avoid unnecessary harm, providing for a measure of individual liberty, respecting persons, promoting internal and external communal security. Consider this claim: There *should be* fundamental differences in the moral standards of different societies." This is a *normative* way of asserting the theory of *ethical relativism.*

• How might the theory of ethical relativism be defended? Be careful though; to defend this view would be to argue that certain normative principles transcend any given society and apply to all of them—ethical relativism, itself, being one example. But if that is so, then ethical relativism implies a self-contradiction.

• How does one determine the behavioral consequences or applicability of ethical relativism? For example, how many persons must agree with an alternative principle before it is considered operative for a given group?

• To criticize a society and urge meaningful social change, one must presume an *external* standard of morality against which the standards of a given society are measured and evaluated. How could one rationally argue for social reform if ethical relativism were true?

M-3 CLASSIFYING NORMATIVE THEORIES

Question: How can we know normative statements are true or false?

Observation: Normative theories differ in terms of how each approaches the question of the meanings of such terms as right, wrong, good, and bad.

Assumption: To Be Knowable Values Must Be Facts of Some Kind

Suppose Values Can Be Defined in Terms of Facts. Those theories which maintain that value words can be defined in terms of either natural or extranatural facts are known as *definist normative theories*. In a *definist* theory, normative statements such as "free sex is wrong" take on truth values; that is, they can be considered to be either true or false.

Some definist theories, called *naturalistic*, define "good" in terms of properties (of things, actions, states of consciousness, or states of affairs) that *can be sensed or commonly observed by ordinary and natural means*. Examples include pleasure, happiness, evolutionary progress, technological progress, self-interest, social mores, economic value.

Other definist theories, called *transcendental*, define "good" in terms of properties (of actions, intentions, persons, states of affairs) that *cannot be known by natural means*, but can be known through extranatural, supernatural, or transcendental means, such as inspiration or immediate revelation from God.

Definist theories are generally criticized for making the logical leap from what is the case to what ought to be the case. For example, technological progress is valued, therefore technological progress ought to be valued. (This same general error is sometimes called "the *is* to *ought* fallacy" or "the naturalistic fallacy.")

Suppose Values Cannot Be Defined in Terms of Facts. Although agreeing that to be knowable values must be facts of some kind, *noncognitivist normative theories* maintain that value words cannot be defined in terms of facts. As a result, it is impossible to know if statements using those words are true or false.

Some noncognitive theories, called *nihilistic*, maintain that the entire moral enterprise is meaningless. Thus, such words as *right* and *good* have no significance and are of no genuine use; in fact, statements employing those words are nonsensical.

Other noncognitive theories, called *emotivist*, maintain that statements asserting moral judgments are to be interpreted as expressions of one's own feelings regarding an action or state of affairs or as more or less sophisticated ways of trying to arouse or evoke similar feelings in others.

Noncognitive theories are generally criticized because they rule out the possibility of moral knowledge. They deny that value judgments can have objectivity. They make efforts to achieve intersubjective agreement on moral

37

matters seem irrational. And, ultimately, they make it illogical to engage in such activities as ascribing moral praise or moral blame or comparing and contrasting alternative courses of action on moral grounds.

Alternative Assumption: To Be Knowable Values Need Not Be Facts

Some normative theories, faced with the apparent dilemma of choosing between the definist or noncognitivist approach, reject the assumption that value words must be associated with facts in order to be knowable. Instead they argue that values can be known even though they cannot be known in the way that facts can be.

These theories, called *nonfactual normative theories,* claim that one can know what value words mean either by appealing to the directly knowable *normative characteristics of things, actions, or persons* or by relying on a *special cognitive ability* specifically oriented toward achieving normative knowledge. For example, some theories ascribe intrinsic normative characteristics to actions on the basis of principles such as the categorical imperative (see E-3). Other theories assert special cognitive abilities, such as *ethical intuition,* which enables us to identify moral characteristics as simple, unanalyzable properties of things.

Areas for Further Inquiry

• Violating a definition ordinarily involves one in a manifest self-contradiction (For example, "I'm talking to three women who are biologically sisters, but they have no siblings.") Yet saying something like, "I know destroying other people's property violates social norms, but it is not always wrong," does not seem to be self-contradictory. In what sense can we *know* examples like these are true?

• If normative knowledge is special in any sense, what is the nature of this special kind of knowledge? How is objectivity or intersubjective verifiability of moral claims possible? How can alternative ethical positions be reconciled?

M-4   CRITICIZING NORMATIVE THEORIES

Question: Why are some criticisms more telling than others?

Observation: Sometimes a criticism seems particularly devastating; at other times a criticism seems beside the point.

Sample Internal Criticisms

Utilitarianism (see E-2) is often criticized for failing to meet *its own standards:*

- of practical applicability because it is impossible to calculate some of the features of pleasure or happiness that must be measurable if the theory is to work;

- of achieving the general good because it fails to recognize the organic interconnectedness of states of affairs will alter the intensity of the pleasure and happiness people experience and because it fails to recognize that the general good is not equivalent to the sum of all individual goods;

- of objectivity because it fails to come to agreement on which states of consciousness are intrinsically valuable.

The approach of defining ethical duties in terms of the categorical imperative (see E-3) is also often criticized for failing to meet *its own standards:*

- of the logical equivalence of the three categorical imperative formulations because in some cases the same action can be interpreted as a duty under one but morally wrong under another and because it is possible to universalize principles (following the first formulation) that do not treat people as intrinsically valuable (violating the second formulation);

- of clarity because the three formulations are underdirective—when the intuitive sense of what our duties are differs between people, no way of resolving those intuitive differences is provided;

- of equivalence because conflicts of duties can arise between alternative formulations of the categorical imperatives. Thus no matter what a person does, he can be blamed for knowingly violating a duty.

The good-life approach (see E-5) is often criticized for failing to meet *its own standards:*

- of applicability because the approach is underdirective. It tells us how to look at life in general, but it fails to give us specific criteria so we know what to do in our day-to-day moral decisions;

- of helpfulness because in characterizing "the good life" or the "life of virtue" it specifies formal criteria that tell us how to maximize the good life but not material criteria for what the good life really amounts to;

- of clarity because of disagreements between theorists regarding paradigm examples of persons who are living (or have lived) the good life and how those model lives are to be interpreted. For example, should I live like Jesus, like the Buddha, like Rev. Martin Luther King, Jr., like Gandhi, like Broadway Joe, or like James "007" Bond?

Two Basic Kinds of Criticisms.   The criticisms listed above have one thing in common. They all aim to show how a theory fails to live up to its own standards of success. This kind of criticism is saying that even if you were an insider and wanted to accept this theory, you would still have serious problems. Such criticism is called *internal* because it originates from within the context of the theory itself.

External criticism, in contrast, asserts that a given theory fails to measure up to a standard which persons who support the theory *do not* necessarily accept. This kind of criticism is saying that your theory fails to measure up to some set of external standards or criteria which you may or may not regard as reasonable and appropriate.

Internal criticisms are the most devastating to a philosophical theory since these *imply that the theory fails to meet its own expectations, standards, or criteria for success.* By contrast, supporters of a given theory may acknowledge the accuracy of an external criticism yet regard the criticism as less important because they do not accept the external criteria it is based on. To see how external criticism works, consider the following examples.

Sample External Criticisms

Let's begin by distinguishing two kinds of ethical theories: those that focus on the consequences of an action to tell if the action is right or wrong, and those that focus on the nature of the action itself, regardless of its consequences. The first kinds of theories are often called *consequentialist.* These theories evaluate the normative characteristics of any given action in terms of the results it will produce. For example, paying taxes is instrumentally valuable because it will advance social utility. Obeying traffic laws is good because it means not getting tickets and not having to pay fines. The second kind of theories are called *deontological.* They evaluate the normative value of an action in terms of its intrinsic characteristics. For example, paying taxes and obeying traffic laws are good because obeying the law is one's moral duty as a responsible member of society.

Those who focus on the intrinsic value of an action (deontologists) externally criticize those who focus on instrumental values (consequentialists) for failing to account for the place of intention in judging the morality of an action and not regarding persons as having intrinsic value. These external criticisms assert that consequentialist theories fail to measure up to standards set by deontologists.

Those who focus on instrumental values criticize those who focus on intrinsic values for proposing that the consequences of an action are not relevant in determining the moral worth of that action. That is, deontologist theories do not measure up on consequentialist criteria.

Good-life or virtue theories (see E-5) externally criticize both consequentialist and deontological theories for being overly concerned with individual actions and failing to see the place judgment and experience have in making moral decisions. In turn, virtue theories are also criticized for being soft on attending to one's moral obligations and for not considering general social utility but only one's own personal fulfillment.

Areas for Further Inquiry

• Criticism is not the last word. Beside counterattacking the opponent's theory, one can respond to criticisms by showing that they are not well founded or by making refinements in one's own position. The give and take between critic and advocate is what makes for precision, progress, and improvement in philosophical theories. (See P-3.) How would you refine the theory you live by from criticisms registered against it? The only wrong answer would be thinking there are no reasonable criticisms.

• Suppose it became clear that cheating was the only way a person could overcome a very difficult obstacle that the person needed to surmount to get their _____. (Fill in the blank with teaching credential, high school diploma, medical degree, real estate license, promotion, or anything of worth.) Considering the values of self-interest, social utility, honesty, respect for persons, conventional and natural rights and duties, moral integrity, and living a meaningful life, what would you advise this person to do if you were giving sound moral advice?

• In view of the ethical theories in E-1 through E-4 as well as the criticisms listed in this section, what is your considered opinion with regard to the following statements:

1. Persons who are awarded a high school diploma but who cannot read at or above the eighth-grade level shall have the legal right to sue the high school district, the local board of education, and individual teachers for damages due to educational malpractice and negligence.

2. In order to achieve a closer approximation to the proportional distribution of persons of different races and sexes in the community, all public employers should immediately implement a vigorous program of reverse discrimination aimed at favoring female and minority candidates for employment and promotion opportunities.

3. To insure the public safety, save taxpayers money, and protect persons from their own irrational choices, smoking in public places shall be illegal, and all persons who ride in or on a motorized vehicle using the public streets or highways must use seat belts and protective helmets. The penalty for each violation shall be ninety days in prison or $500.

FREEDOM

F-1   FREEDOM AND CAUSALITY

Question: How can we reconcile our awareness of free choice with our basic belief in the pervasive character of causality?

Dilemma: We have a problem. If people are not free, we cannot hold them morally responsible for what they do. But if free choice is an uncaused event, then the principle of universal causality, on which all of science is founded, is not true.

A Challenging Set of Statements

Consider these statements and ask yourself in turn if each is true:

1. All human choices are events.

2. Every event has a cause.

3. Anything that is caused is not free.

4. Some human choices are free.

5. It is reasonable to hold people morally responsible for what they do only if their choices are free.

Now consider the implications of combining some of these statements. For example, it follows from the truth of 1, 2, and 3 that 4 must be false. In other words, if the first three statements are true, then

42

6. No human choices are free.

From 6 and 5 it follows that:

7. People should not be held morally responsible for what they do.

We might want to reject 7 because it is contrary to our moral intuitions to think that people can never be held morally accountable. But to reject 7, we must get rid of either 6 or 5. Since 5 seems like a reasonable assumption, let's consider rejecting 6.

Given that we have a contradiction between 6 and 4, we must reject one or the other of them anyway; so, why not reject 6. This means we can keep 4: Some human choices are free. So far so good, but to keep 4, we must also discard one of the first three numbered statements since together they logically imply that 4 is false. Since each seems true, which one should we deny?

Our other choice is to reject 4. This way we can keep 1, 2, and 3. Of course this implies that 6 is true. And if 6 is true, we seem forced to the undesirable conclusion that 7 is true also.

Let's go through this reasoning once more.

A Look at the Alternatives

The first alternative: Suppose we reject 6 and say that some human choices are free. Now we must discard 1, 2, or 3. But 1 and 3 seem to be true almost as a matter of definition. The only real candidate for rejection seems to be 2: Every event has a cause. Maybe there are *uncaused events,* and free human choices are examples of them. This strategy allows us also to hang onto 5 and reject 7, thus permitting us to hold people morally responsible for what they freely choose to do. Our problem, and unfortunately it's a big one, is how to explain "uncaused events"! This strategy seems to salvage the idea of human morality but to be in deep water scientifically. It is called *libertarianism.* (See F-2.)

The second alternative: Suppose we reject 4 and say that no human choices are free. If we do that, we can keep 2, every event has a cause, along with 1 and 3. Our problem is that even if we still hang onto 5 we are stuck with the idea that people cannot be held morally responsible for what they do because they could not have acted freely. This strategy seems to make scientific sense while rendering ethics completely pointless. It is called *hard determinism.* (See F-3.)

A Third Possibility?

Suppose we start from the other side and say that the scientific concept of causality must somehow be compatible with the practice of holding people morally responsible for what they freely choose to do. This means that we will try to find a way to make the principle of universal scientific causality compatible with the concept of human moral freedom. To achieve this, we must explore, and maybe adjust, the precise meaning of *event* or *human choice* or *free* or *cause*. If the adjustments turn out to be arbitrary stipulations that neither scientists nor ethical theorists can agree with, then our efforts will have been futile. But if not, then perhaps we will have escaped a nasty dilemma. This difficult choice is known as *compatibilism* or *soft determinism*. (See F-4.)

Areas for Further Inquiry

• To say a person did X freely, in the morally relevant sense, is to say that the person could have decided to do something other than X. Must a choice be scientifically uncaused in order for us to consider it free in the morally relevant sense?

• Before looking ahead to the next three sections, what arguments do you suppose could be most reasonably advanced for and against each of the three alternative positions sketched briefly above? Are there any more alternatives?

• A key assumption, statement 5, operates throughout the *freedom* sections: It is reasonable to hold people morally responsible for what they do only if their choices are free. But how accurate is this assumption? Are there cases when we hold people morally responsible for things that clearly were not done freely? Are there cases when we do not hold people morally responsible for things that they did freely?

F-2   LIBERTARIANISM

Question: How do we explain the fact of human freedom?

Proposal: Given that holding people morally responsible for acts they freely choose to perform is reasonable and appropriate, the agenda is, therefore, to explain human freedom and set limits on so-called universal causality.

An Argument for Libertarianism

As human beings, we have all experienced deliberation. Deliberation involves confronting alternatives between which we must choose. When we deliberate, we consider reasons and select one alternative over another. After that, we act on the basis of that decision. So, at such times humans are self-determining agents. The acts of self-determining agents are not events in causal chains. Thus, some events—specifically human decisions—do not have causes.

Some thinkers distinguish sharply between *acts* and *events*. Acts come about on account of *reasons* and *decisions*, but events come about because of the presence of antecedent sufficient *causes*. Acts are *performed* by *agents*. Events *happen* because the *conditions* for their occurrence exist. An alternative way to state the libertarian conclusion would be: The principle that every event has a cause does not apply to free human acts.

Are Free Acts Random and Without Origins?

"I'm not convinced," the critic might say. "If free acts or acts of self-determination are uncaused, then they are *unexplainable* and have the appearance of unpredictable random events. But it is unreasonable to hold persons accountable for random, unpredictable behavior. So, your approach still fails to achieve its main purpose, which is to justify holding people morally responsible for what they do. Besides, you make freedom seem mysterious. What is it about human beings that generates a free human act? Don't our decisions occur in our brains?"

Products of Habit and Will

The Libertarian might reply, "Free acts need not be considered random. They are the fruit of years of experience, habit, temperament, education, prior decisions, goals, desires, and disposition, which—taken together—form our *personality* or *character*. As mature people, we can act in accordance with character, or we can decide to break with our past and strike out in new directions. If you must identify the source of our free acts, then why not say free acts are the products of human volition. Call them acts of the will, if you wish."

Explanations Put Off But Not Accomplished

"You really haven't answered my questions," the critic might complain. "Where did one's character come from? Things like habits and temperaments do not arise in a causal vacuum. Nor do so-called breaks with our past. Either such things are random, or they are caused. In either case, holding people responsible for them seems unreasonable. And about the so-called will— either the will is a part of the brain or it is not. If it is, then an act of the will is a biochemical event in one's brain. As such, it is a physical event and part of a causal chain. If the will is not part of the brain or some other physical part of the body, what is it and how does it make a physical thing, the body, move and do things?"

Freedom as a Basic Fact of Human Experience

"I understand your objection," a Libertarian could assert, "but it only shows how stubbornly people cling to naive belief in universal causality. No matter what reply I give, you will say, 'What caused that?' But at some point the principle of causality itself must come up for review. As to the specifics of your objections, certainly people can be held responsible for their habits and for other elements that go into making up their character. That's what training and education are all about!

"But I want you to stop arguing and reflect for a moment on your own experience. If you do, you'll see that freedom is a basic fact. We know that we do not have to act in accordance with habit, temperament, prior decisions, or anything else. That is what it means to be free.

"As to the details of whether the will is a part of a person's brain or not, what practical difference could that possibly make? If you must, say that the will is a power of the human mind. The questions of how the mind and body interact, or if the mind is the same as the brain, take us into highly debated areas of metaphysics. But people know some things for certain. They know what *deliberation* feels like. They also know what *temptation, remorse, regret, guilt,* and *pride of achievement* feel like. Above all, these experiences feel as if they did not occur because of outside causes. And these common human experiences are not illusions either. So, whatever metaphysical theory is used to account for them— brain events or acts of the mind—the theory must take into account the *certainty of these immediate experiences.*"

Areas for Further Inquiry

• Does libertarianism force one into certain views regarding human nature and reality? (See N-1 "The Mind-Body Problem" and N-3 "Metaphysical Idealism.")

• If libertarianism is true, what are the implications for public policy and personal ethics? Specifically, if human choices are unexplainable and unpredictable in the final analysis, what justifications would there be for punishment and praise or for legislating incentives and deterrents?

Philosophical Role Playing

What more might the critic say to counter the libertarian?

F-3   HARD DETERMINISM

Question: How do we apply the concept of causality to human behavior?

Claim: Although people might think they act freely, they are mistaken or unaware of the true physical or psychological causes of their so-called free choices.

An Argument for Hard Determinism

Everything that happens has a causal ancestry extending in-definitely into the past. Even if called acts of the will, human choices are events that happen at specific times and places. As events, human choices have causes. So, human choices are not free. It is unreasonable to hold people responsible unless they are free. Thus, talk of freedom and responsibility is misguided and should be replaced with talk of conditioning and behavior modification.

How Scientifically Accurate Is
This View of Causality?

"You've made a crucial mistake," the critic might point out. "Your description of scientific causality isn't factual. Some natural events are random. Consider, for example, the decay of radioactive material. Although science can predict the general rate of decay, it cannot accurately predict which particles or exactly how many of them will decay at any specific moment in time. Or consider predictions about the behavior of large aggregate groups. Social scientists can predict within certain limits the behavior of large numbers of people regarding certain kinds of issues (e.g., market behavior regarding product acceptance). However, social scientists cannot predict the behavior of any individual person regarding that same issue. So, not every event has a cause."

An advocate of hard determinism might persist, "Granted, the concept of causality is more complex than at first it appeared. (See N-8.) Science can still proceed with the effort to identify the conditions antecedent to the occurrence of an event. When those are properly identified and understood, we can explain and predict the event within certain limits and ranges of accuracy. Your objection does not imply that events have no causes, although it does correctly reflect that, in certain kinds of cases, predictive certainty cannot be achieved."

Results and the Burden of Proof

"Well," the critic might say, "the burden of proof is still on you. If there are causes that scientifically explain each human choice, don't keep them secret. Tell us what they are."

"I would be delighted," the advocate might respond, "but in due time. Remember, the scientific enterprise is only about three hundred years old. Presently, it is pursuing several promising lines of inquiry. One approach is to analyze all human behavior in terms of physical factors such as genetics, environment, physiology, biology, and chemistry. Another strategy approaches human behavior from the psychoanalytic perspective. By first understanding deviant behavior in terms of unconscious causes, we plan eventually to explain all human behavior in the same way."

"Yes, well, after three hundred years of study, one would have hoped for more," the critic might remark. "So far the effort to understand human choices in terms of strictly physical causes has not worked out. Although we might be able to predict what people will do when they are under the influence of certain chemicals, no physicalistic theories as yet yield sound predictions or explanations of normal decision making. And we can't say much more for the psychoanalytic approach. Even if we understand deviant behavior in terms of unconscious psychopathology, the prospects of consistently *predicting* human behavior, even deviant behavior, seem remote. The extension of the psychoanalytic approach to explaining and predicting normal behavior scientifically seems highly unlikely unless conscious human choices are taken into account.

"And I have a final objection as well," the critic might add. "Even if the physical or psychoanalytic approaches were successful, we would need to explain more. For example, suppose a stranger stops me on the street. The physical and psychoanalytic causes of both of us being there could be explained, but I still would not know how to treat the stranger unless I knew more. Specifically, I would need to know the stranger's intentions toward me. Does the stranger want to mug me, proposition me, ask me for assistance, or give me a gift? A complete explanation of human behavior involves more than an analysis of physical and unconscious psychological antecedent conditions. It involves discussions of motives, intentions, reasons, purposes, and goals."

Areas for Further Inquiry

•   Does hard determinism force one into certain views regarding human nature and reality? (See N-1 "The Mind-Body Problem" and N-2 "Metaphysical Materialism.")

•   If hard determinism is true, then people cannot be held responsible for what they do. What are the implications of this for public policy? What would it be like to live in a community where people could not be held responsible for what they did? What justifications would there be for legislation regarding punishment and economic incentives or deterrents?

Philosophical Role Playing

As a hard determinist, how might you reply to the critic's objection about the need to reference motives and so on in explaining human behavior?

F-4   COMPATIBILISM

Question: How do we reconcile universal causality with the sound practice of holding people responsible for their free actions?

Insight: The key consideration in holding people morally responsible for their actions is whether they could have acted in ways other than they did.

An Argument for Compatibilism

Everything has a cause, but that does not mean predictions about exactly how things will turn out are always possible. Human choices are sometimes free, but that does not mean they are random, unpredictable, or unexplainable. It is reasonable to hold a person morally responsible for her or his choices if the person could have acted otherwise. In many cases, a person makes a given choice but could have made a different one. So, in many cases, people can be held morally responsible for their choices.

The *compatibilist* position is also known as *soft determinism*. In its classical form, it emphasizes freedom of the will and freedom from coercion. In its more recent forms, known as *compatibilism*, it emphasizes freedom in the sense of making rational and unconstrained choices.

The Meaning of caused and free

The challenge of any middle-ground position is that it must respond to criticisms from all directions. Curious about the concept of causality operating here, one critic might ask about the justification for the opening sentence in the argument above. Another might question the meaning of *free* in the second sentence by asking whether *free* is intended to be synonymous with *unconstrained.* If the answer is affirmative, then the critic might go on to say, "Well, we have a problem, then. A choice might be *free* in the sense of not being subject to external constraints, but the choice might still only be a manifestation of compulsive behavior. As such, it is not free in the morally relevant sense. People cannot be held responsible for compulsive behavior even if they were not coerced into it or did it while being unconstrained."

The advocate of compatibilism would probably be prepared for both kinds of questions. To the first, regarding the justification of the idea that everything is caused, the advocate might assert, "Two kinds of cases are relevant here. One is purely a matter of physics. Although physicists can predict the general rate of decay of radioactive material, they cannot accurately predict which molecules and how many of them will decay at any specific moment in time. The problem is not one of technology but of relating to the behavior of radioactive material in principle. The second case involves human choices, but it does not beg the question. In certain cases, social scientists can predict within limits the behavior of large aggregates of people, (e.g., voting patterns). However, social scientists cannot predict how any specific person is actually going to vote."

To the second question, regarding the meaning of *free,* the advocate of compatibilism might maintain, "The morally relevant sense of *free* is the one given in the third sentence. It goes beyond unconstrained and includes the concept of acting rationally. That means, prior to making a decision one identifies one's goals and the alternative ways of achieving those goals, anticipates and evaluates the consequences of each alternative, considers—if necessary—developing additional alternatives or modifying one's goals. Finally one makes a decision regarding that goal and how best to achieve it, with the reasons for selecting that way of acting rather than other ways in which she could have acted clearly in mind."

Areas for Further Inquiry

• If *morally free* means *rational and unconstrained,* can a person be *conditioned* or trained to be free?

• It seems possible to be rational about being rational. That is, one could rationally decide that in certain kinds of situations he or she will sit down and deliberate before acting. What causes a person to decide to deliberate? If an answer to that question exists, does it imply that hard determinism is true after all? If people can be rational about being rational, does this suggest that we can hold people morally responsible for whether they act rationally?

• Does compatibilism force one into certain views regarding human nature and reality? (See N-1 "The Mind-Body Problem" and N-4 "Metaphysical Dualism.")

• Section F-3 stresses the scientific basis for a denial of human freedom. A different argument might be developed out of the considerations in R-3 "The Problem of Freedom." It would be based on the idea that if an all-knowing or an all-powerful creator exists, then humans could not be free. Is human freedom compatible with God's existence?

• If compatibilism is true, what implications would this hold for public policy and personal ethics? How does the concept of rational action relate to moral autonomy? Should governments have the right to limit human freedom either by constraining choices or limiting the information vital to rational deliberation? If so, what limits and why?

Philosophical Role Playing

Greater specificity is given to the idea of unconstrained, rational action in F-5 "The Concept of Autonomy." But for now, how would a compatibilist reply to a critic who demands clarification of these terms?

F-5   THE CONCEPT OF AUTONOMY

Question: What are the specific conditions under which a person can be said to be an autonomous individual?

Stipulation: Autonomy means acting rationally and without constraint.

The First Condition for Autonomy: Rational *Decision Making*

Decision making cannot be called *rational* unless it follows certain necessary procedural steps. These include:

1. establishing goals and objectives and placing them in order of priority,
2. identifying alternative means to achieve one's goals and objectives,
3. anticipating, to a reasonable extent, all the probable and possible consequences, whether intended or unintended, of each means,
4. assessing those consequences,
5. selecting the means that can achieve the goals and objectives without also producing unacceptable consequences.
6. If there are none to choose from in 5, trying to develop more alternatives or reconsidering one's goals and objectives,
7. and evaluating the results of one's decision with a view toward doing a better job of rational decision making in the future.

Decision making cannot be called *rational* unless the process described above is not influenced, diverted, or prevented from reaching its natural outcome by extraneous internal or external limitations or considerations.

• Examples of extraneous internal limitations or considerations: emotionalism, prejudice, indecisiveness, lack of interest, lack of attention, inability to infer consequences, ignorance of relevant available data, mental laziness, lack of creativity, and inability to make normative assessments.

• Examples of extraneous external limitations or considerations: distractions, unavailability of relevant data, forced ignorance or denial of relevant education and training, reliance on trusted but inaccurate information, and insufficient time or energy to deliberate fully.

The Second Condition for Autonomy: Unconstrained *Decision Making*

Decision making cannot be called *unconstrained* unless:

1. There are sufficient resources such as funds, transportation, com-

51

munications, personnel, equipment, opportunity, time, and so forth, with which to consider or carry out specific alternatives.

2. There are no coercive obstacles, legal or illegal, that others place in the way of deliberation or execution of alternatives, such as physiological, physical, social, or economic barriers, psychological or physical threats, and so on.

3. There are no psychological or biological limitations—such as mental illness, physical disability, ill health, immaturity, weakness, drunkenness, chemical interference, and so on—either natural, accidental, or deliberately induced that prevent acting on certain alternatives.

Positive and Negative Freedom

Historically philosophers have used the phrases "positive freedom" and "negative freedom" in discussing the use of coercive force or the exercise of personal liberties. Traditionally *negative freedom* has been defined as being *free-from* coercive limitations or, more broadly, *being unconstrained*. *Positive freedom* was often characterized as *freedom-to* exercise one's liberties or rights. In practice, however, *freedom-to* translated into limiting the powers of others, specifically the government, so that the person could pursue his interests without constraints. In effect, *freedom-to* was only an alternative way of saying *freedom-from*. More recent analyses of positive freedom equate it with *being rational*.

Areas for Further Inquiry

• Should a person be forced to become more rational? Is this a justification for compulsory education?

• To what extent is a person responsible for trying to maximize one's own opportunities for rational decision making and minimize the chances of being constrained; that is, for creating one's positive freedom and preserving one's negative freedom?

• Given the more recent analyses of *positive freedom*, in what sense is America the "land of the free?" When someone is a "freedom fighter," does that imply they are fighting only for *negative freedom* or might they not also be fighting for *positive freedom?*

• What is the relationship between autonomy and moral responsibility? Is it true that if a person acts autonomously, then the person is morally responsible? Conversely, is it true that if a person is morally responsible, then the person is acting autonomously?

Philosophical Role Playing

Compatibilists, libertarians, and hard determinists would give very different answers to many of these questions. From your understanding of each position (see F-2, F-3, and F-4), anticipate their answers.

F-6   THE CONCEPT OF RESPONSIBILITY

Question: What is the conceptual relationship between autonomy and moral responsibility?

Thesis: If the morally relevant sense of freedom *is unconstrained, rational choice, then a person is morally responsible if she or he acted autonomously.*

An Argument That Autonomy Implies Responsibility

Saying a choice is *free* means it is made rationally and without constraint. Any action taken rationally and without constraint is, by definition, autonomous. (See F-5.) It is unreasonable to hold people morally responsible for their choices unless they are free choices. So, if a person acts autonomously, then the person is morally responsible for his or her actions.

Hard Determinist and Libertarian Objections

An advocate of hard determinism might object: "The first sentence imposes conditions that are too strong. Nobody is ever in the position to satisfy both those conditions because nobody can escape causality and act any way except how they actually do act."

A libertarian might register the opposite objection. "The first sentence is too weak. An act can satisfy both these conditions but still not really be free, that is, uncaused. But a person is not morally responsible for an unfree act even if the definition of autonomous is satisfied."

Exploration.   How would you defend the above argument from each of these two criticisms? Are there other objections to consider?

An Argument That Responsibility Does Not Imply Autonomy

A person can deliberate about being rational and can take steps to be more rational. A person can also anticipate problems and take steps to remove some of the potential constraints to rational decision making. So, to some degree, a person can be held responsible for achieving and maintaining autonomy. From this it follows that failing to act autonomously does not relieve a person of moral responsibility. In other words, you can be held morally responsible even if you failed to act with the fullest possible autonomy!

Exploration. If this argument is logically strong and its premises are true, then it is right to hold people responsible for failing to educate themselves, failing to think things through, and wasting opportunities to achieve deeper and broader understandings of life that enhance rationality. Do you agree that people have these moral obligations?

However, if this argument is not sound, then it would seem irrational to hold people morally responsible for accidents that occur due to their negligence, lack of planning, foresight, or information, and so on. To what extent, if any, is it reasonable to relieve people of moral accountability in such cases?

In view of your responses to the above—and given your understandings of one's actual *legal* liabilities—how are legal liabilities and moral responsibilities related?

Philosophical Role Playing

Considering the views of libertarians (see F-2), hard determinists (see F-3), and compatibilists (see F-4), what might some of their objections and replies be to the second argument? How might representatives of each of the three theories reply to the questions you were asked in the "Exploration" section above?

F-7 THEORIES OF PUNISHMENT AND PRAISE

Question: When is praise and when is punishment appropriate?

Conjecture: Praise and punishment should generally, but not exclusively, be connected to moral responsibility.

An Argument Based on the Intrinsic Value of Persons

Treating people with respect implies giving them what they deserve. People responsible for doing well deserve praise. People responsible for misbehaving deserve punishment. So, praise and punishment are justified in terms of the demands of respecting persons as intrinsically valuable in themselves.

This argument gives support to the *retributive theory* of punishment, which considers punishment as intrinsically right regardless of its consequences. This general approach views punishment as any one of four or more things: a form of repayment, revenge for an injury, a form of respect for the criminal as an autonomous person, or a way of restoring the social balance between persons that the criminal has disrupted. (See M-2 for the distinction between intrinsic and instrumental.)

An Argument from Consideration of Consequences

Praising people is a form of conditioning that can and does lead them to repeat desired actions. Punishing criminals can and does lead them to reconsider their ways of acting and not resume their criminal activities. Knowing the policies of praise and punishment can and does lead others in society to do things that earn praise and refrain from doing things that earn punishment. So, praise and punishment are justified on instrumental grounds in terms of the desirable consequences they produce.

This argument gives support to the *preventive theory* of punishment, which maintains that imprisonment or capital punishment are ways to keep society safe from criminals. This argument also gives support to the *deterrent theory*, which sees praise as an incentive and punishment as a deterrent to influence the behavior not only of the individual involved but also of others in society. For the deterrent theory to be effective, the policy of punishment must be known to be swift and sure. The consequentialist approach is also used to justify the *rehabilitative theory* of punishment, which has as its goal returning the criminal to society as a contributing member.

Areas for Further Inquiry

• What is the plausibility of *revenge* or *respect for the criminal* as moral grounds for a social policy calling for capital punishment? (See E-3 "Categorical Imperatives.")

• Are each of the premise statements in the second argument—the one based on the consideration of consequences—actually true? If any one is false, can the argument be salvaged? Which consequentialist theory of punishment is associated with each premise? Are the goals of deterrence, rehabilitation, and protection actually achieved? If so, at what human and economic cost? (See E-2 "Social Utility.")

Philosophical Role Playing

What would advocates of libertarianism, hard determinism, and compatibilism say about the retributive, preventive, deterrent, and rehabilitative theories of punishment?

GOVERNMENT

G-1 THE CONCEPT OF JUSTICE

Question: What is justice?

Analysis: In the most basic sense, justice has to do with the fair distribution of benefits and burdens among persons under conditions of relative scarcity and conflict of interest.

Three Conditions for Questions of Justice to Arise

1. The issues at hand must concern the distribution of benefits (e.g., money, resources, prerogatives, opportunities, material goods, rewards, services) or the distribution of burdens (e.g., work, taxes, fees, obligations, duties, responsibilities, liabilities, punishments).

2. In terms of the distributions of benefits, there must be *relative scarcity*. That is, a greater demand for the benefit must exist than the supply of benefits can accommodate (e.g., not enough food, medical care, scholarships, so forth for all who need or deserve those things).

3. An *incompatibility* or *conflict of interests* must exist among those who would and could benefit or among those who could and should be burdened (e.g., more deserving students than scholarships available, more people needing specialized medical care than can be provided, more candidates for promotion than positions to be filled, more workers available than tasks to be assigned, more criminals to be punished than jail cells to house them).

Proportionality and Relevance

• For a resolution to be considered just, it must be *universalizable*. (See E-3.) That is, whatever the basis used for making the decision about the distribution of benefits and burdens, that basis must apply to all interested persons *without reference to morally irrelevant considerations*.

• For a resolution to be considered just, it must make distributions of burdens and benefits to individuals *in proportion* to their needs or merits. It is not considered just to overburden some or to give others more benefits than they deserve.

• Conditions over which persons have no control are generally, but not always, ruled out as the basis for the distribution of benefits or burdens because these conditions are considered morally irrelevant (e.g., age, sex, race, and other physical characteristics that are genetically based or happenstances of historical or social situation).

• In terms of rewards and punishments, for a distribution to be considered just, rewards must go to those who bring about things of positive value, and the punishments must go to those who bring about things of negative value.

Compensatory Justice, Retributive Justice, and Distributive Justice

• *Compensatory justice* is a corrective distribution of benefits to persons who have been denied deserved benefits or have suffered undeserved hardships. (E.g., programs of affirmative action are intended to compensate for the unfair discriminatory employment practices of prior years.)

• *Retributive justice* is a corrective distribution of burdens to persons who have undeservedly enjoyed benefits or were morally culpable for failing to fulfill their responsibilities. (E.g., legal penalties and fines are generally intended to be retributive.)

• *Distributive justice* is the distribution of burdens and benefits to persons under conditions of relative scarcity and conflict of interest. (E.g., deciding which of too many applicants will be admitted to the entering class in medical school is a question of finding a fair distribution for a limited number of benefits.)

Justice and Moral Responsibility

In cases of *compensatory justice* and *retributive justice*, the issue of moral responsibility is crucial. If compensation or retribution is to be made, the question of who should bear the costs (burdens) of either providing that compensation or suffering that retribution arises. When and where possible, assigning such burdens to those morally responsible for creating the initial inequity is considered highly appropriate.

57

Formal Justice

The basic concept of distributive justice is *to treat relevantly similar persons similarly in proportion to their relevant similarities* and *to treat relevantly different persons differently in proportion to their relevant differences*. (E.g., children of comparable age, training, and athletic abilities are given the opportunity to compete against each other in an athletic tournament. However, those with demonstrably superior or inferior strength, maturity, or training opportunities are barred from that competition, but they are allowed to participate in other competitive groupings that are formed taking into account their relevant differences and similarities.)

Areas for Further Inquiry

•   The formal principle of distributive justice does not tell us which bases for the distribution of benefits and burdens are the morally relevant ones in any given case. But, in day-to-day situations, knowing which considerations are relevant is essential to actually making a just decision. What might some of those considerations be? (The distinction here, between *formal* and *material* justice, is like the distinction between *formal* and *material* virtues in E-5.)

•   At times people say that treating people *equally* is the same as treating them *justly*. But the discussion above suggests that the distribution of benefits and burdens *need not, and probably should not, be equal to be just*. What is the relationship between equality and justice?

Philosophical Role Playing

Consider the case of admitting students to medical school. Assume that many more candidates apply than there are places available. In terms of the concept of distributive justice, how would you propose deciding which students should be admitted? In other words, what would you propose as the *material* considerations that are relevant in making a fair and just decision? Now add the concepts of compensatory and retributive justice. Are there reasonable claims that can be made by specific candidates or groups of candidates that they should or should not be given favored treatment on compensatory or retributive grounds?

G-2   THE CONCEPT OF EQUALITY

Question: On a conceptual level, how do equality and the formal principle of justice (presented in G-1) relate?

Reflection: Treating everyone equally may not always be the just thing to do.

Equality and Material Principles of Justice

Consider the case of John and Marsha: both work for the same company and perform the same basic job. Marsha has been with the company ten years; John, only five. It is time for their annual raises. Marsha proposes that "treating them equally" means she should get twice as big a raise as John because she has been there twice as long. John protests that since he supervises eight people but Marsha supervises only six, "treating them equally" means his raise must be 25 percent greater than hers.

In this case, appealing to the rhetoric of equal treatment only obscures the real issue, which is deciding on the morally relevant consideration to use in distributing annual raises. *When talk of "equal treatment" is a disguised way of smuggling a proposed material criteria of justice into a discussion about the distribution of benefits and burdens, then equality and formal justice are not the same thing.*

Extending the case, their superior determines that she will review the quality of their job performances to decide each one's raise. Thus, the *material* criterion to be used to distribute benefits in this case has been decided upon. Then the superior declares, "I will treat you equally. That is, the distribution for both of you will be based on the *same relevant consideration,* and I will give you each a raise *in proportion* to your achievements on that criterion."

In so doing, the superior is defining "equal treatment" in the same way that *formal justice* was defined in G-1. *When "equal treatment" means formal justice, then equality and justice are definitionally the same.*

Egalitarianism

Extending the case, a union official objects to the superior's proposal. The union official says that "equal treatment" means all workers, regardless of how well they performed on the job, should get the same raise. Management refuses on the grounds that such an "egalitarian" approach would be harmful to productivity.

Egalitarianism is the theory that all persons, *simply because they are persons,* should share exactly equally in all benefits and all burdens that are to be distributed. Objections to egalitarianism usually stress that the equal (nonproportional) distribution of wealth and responsibilities would lead to unwelcome results. The more expensive needs of some people (e.g., major medical expenses as a result of a catastrophic injury) might not be able to be met. Or deciding things in a strictly egalitarian way would place some persons in positions of responsibility for which they are clearly unprepared and unqualified (let's all take our turn being president!).

In cases where "equal treatment" is a disguised way of proposing the application of the theory of egalitarianism, equality and formal justice are not the same thing.

Areas for Further Inquiry

•   Could a defender of egalitarianism say that benefits should be distributed *in proportion* to need and burdens *in proportion* to abilities? Or would this be the same as abandoning the fundamental principle of egalitarianism, namely that all persons, just because they are persons, should be given equal shares of all benefits and burdens?

•   In some cases, we begin deliberations with the idea that the persons involved are unequal and treating them differently is fair, unless someone can prove that they are equal. (E.g., the starting salary for the president of a corporation is much higher than the starting salary for the office clerk.) In other cases, we begin deliberations by presuming persons are equal, and we treat them equally unless someone can prove they are not equal. (E.g., all citizens are accorded equal treatment unless one is proven to be guilty of a crime; then that person is punished.) Remembering that each presumption creates a *burden of proof* on those who would disagree, in which kinds of cases is the *presumption of equality* wiser and in which kinds of cases is the *presumption of inequality* wiser?

Philosophical Role Playing

As a philosopher-consultant, imagine you are a "moral arbitrator." How would you resolve the dispute between the union and management in the example of John and Marsha and still preserve justice? In resolving this dispute, you will, of necessity, be proposing certain criteria as the bases for the distribution of raises. These criteria become *material* principles of justice in this particular case. What material principles would you use?

G-3   THE WORK CRITERION AND THE NEED CRITERION

Question: What material criteria should be used to actually decide who deserves benefits and who deserves burdens?

Guiding principle: Where possible, it is reasonable to use criteria over which people have some control; that is, over which they are in some sense responsible.

An Argument for the Work Criterion

Material principles of justice ought to be things over which people have some control and for which they can be held accountable. Work is clearly something a person can be held responsible for doing. Working produces positive results; failing to work produces negative results. Those who produce positive results deserve the benefits they have earned; whereas those who produce negative results deserve the punishments and burdens they have earned. So, work is an excellent candidate to be a material principle of justice.

A Debate over the Work Criterion

CRITIC: "Work is too ambiguous. Do you mean ability, productivity, or effort?"

ADVOCATE: "I mean ability. Let the greatest rewards go to those with the most refined and polished skills such as entertainers, professional athletes, doctors, corporate executives, and so forth."

CRITIC: "If you are saying that a person should be held responsible for developing his or her skills and potentials to their fullest, I agree. In other words, in the distribution of burdens, people who fail to work up to the potential of their ability deserve punishment of some kind. But the rewards for such occupations as those you name reflect the values of our society (e.g., entertainment, health, the social status of various occupations) and not necessarily the degree to which all persons in our society have perfected their own particular abilities. Besides, your original argument was that the material principle of justice should be something over which people have some control. People do not have control over their native abilities, only over the degree to which they develop and use them."

ADVOCATE: "Then let's agree that we are not talking about raw talent, but about refined and perfected skills. And, by the way, I also want to add that actual productivity is also a good criterion. Let's hold people accountable for results—that is, for their actual, not just potential, contributions."

CRITIC: "That will work except in those cases where contributions cannot easily be measured: nursing, education, art, research, human services, entertainment, counseling, the ministry, and the like. How do you measure productivity in these kinds of occupations? What are we going to do when a person's productive activity does not yield easily quantified output?"

ADVOCATE: "In those cases and others, too, we should measure effort."

CRITIC: "We could measure effort in hours, but this doesn't fit every case. What about writers, for example? Moreover, we all know people who try hard but simply cannot produce. So let's be careful here. Otherwise we'll end up with the not so hard working but much more productive people being held responsible for producing the benefits that will go to the less productive but harder working people. The more resources we use to reward those who try hard but don't produce, the less we will have in reserve should a real problem ever arise."

61

An Argument for the Need Criterion

Everyone has the same basic needs. As people, we are all equally deserving of having our basic needs met, and meeting basic human needs is a morally good and right thing to do. Therefore, need is an excellent candidate to be a material principle of justice.

A Debate over the Need Criterion

CRITIC: "People cannot be held responsible for having basic needs. I thought we were looking for criteria over which people had some control."

ADVOCATE: "True, but people can do something about making sure their needs are met. They're not helpless! They're not so completely without control as they would be if we used things like ethnicity, race, age, heritage, or sex as our material criteria."

CRITIC: "The concept of a basic need is complicated. A hierarchy of basic human needs exists, and as one satisfies primitive needs for food and shelter, other levels of needs emerge. Also, needs are related to social circumstances and all sorts of other factors. For example, to obtain the job you want, you might need a college education. If you work far enough from home, you could need a car. But to say that a college education and a car, while not extravagant, are basic human needs is strange, too."

ADVOCATE: "Some societies could not afford to help people meet the kinds of needs you have identified. But others can, or they can give partial support to persons who also invest their own effort in trying to better themselves. For example, relatively inexpensive, open-access, public higher education is one way for society to respond. Low-interest loans, tax credits, and tax deductions are other examples."

CRITIC: "We cannot help everyone with everything they say they need. And in times of trouble, we may not even be able to help anyone."

ADVOCATE: "As resources become more scarce, we can do much less. But that does not change the basic concept of justice. However, public policy is going to have to make choices here since resources are not limitless, and, yes, people always seem to claim they need more than what can be supplied."

Areas for Further Inquiry

• The work criterion has the advantage of connecting the distribution of benefits and burdens most directly to what people earn for themselves. Is there a plausible way to introduce the concept of receiving what you have earned into the discussion about needs?

• There are needs, and there are needs. What assumptions about human nature and the human character does social policy based on the need criterion make? Are those assumptions correct?

• What should the policy be toward people who have been disadvantaged or advantaged by social circumstances over which they had no control (e.g., by attending inadequate schools when they were young)? Presuming that everyone's basic needs count equally, do you agree that a just social policy is one that benefits those who had been disadvantaged through no fault of their own and places the costs of creating those advantages on those who were initially blessed with advantages they did not deserve?

Philosophical Role Playing

The critics and the advocates in the above debates dashed through several ideas rather quickly. In their haste, some important ideas might have been underdeveloped. First as advocate, then as critic, try to refine a reasoned policy with regard to the proper applications and limitations of each of the two proposed material criteria.

G-4   THE THEORY OF ANARCHISM

Question: Should humans, who are by nature social, establish governments?

Presumption: When one group of individuals in a community is given, claims, or can consistently and successfully exercise a monopoly on the use of coercive force, that group can be considered a government and that community can be considered a state.

An Argument for Anarchism

A government is, by definition, one group's exercise of a monopoly on the use of coercive force in a society, including the promulgation and enforcement of rules. It is immoral for one group in society to make and enforce rules over others. To form a state and have a government implies the surrender of one's moral responsibility for one is obligated to follow the rules the government makes. Each individual is morally responsible for his or her own actions and cannot surrender moral responsibility to another. Thus, governments are by nature immoral and should not be formed.

63

Anarchism is based on the theory of *individual sovereignty*. That is, each individual has the ultimate moral authority, not derived from any other source, to live and act as he or she chooses.

A Debate Regarding the Theory of Anarchism

CRITIC: "There are too many positive values associated with communal living to accept anarchism. Without government, there would be chaos!"

ADVOCATE: "That's a common misconception. So let's start off by clarifying what the theory of anarchism is *not* saying. Anarchism does not deny the many positive values of living in a community such as the possibilities this creates for sharing knowledge, wealth, labor and for benefiting from the special talents of each person. Nor does anarchism deny the emotional, psychological, or spiritual advantages of communal living. It is not a rejection of the need for customs, mores, and social norms of behavior or even using negative sanctions (such as shunning, excommunication, withdrawal of property rights) to deter or discourage unacceptable conduct. *Anarchism does not advocate chaos. Anarchism is not essentially antisocial.* In fact, anarchists often place great value on family, companionships, partnerships, joint efforts, trusts, co-ops, and any structures that involve freely deciding to work with others for mutually desirable and beneficial ends. However, anarchists do believe it is unwise, immoral, or unnecessary to vest one group of persons (the government) in a society with *sole* rights to the use of *coercive* power."

CRITIC: "I appreciate your clarifications, but I still have problems. Under the *social contract theory*, governments exist because people have agreed among themselves to surrender some of their individual prerogatives in order to form a government that will insure their fundamental human needs are met. So, forming a government is not immoral. On the contrary, it's the rational thing to do."

ADVOCATE: "Let's not forget that the social contract theory should not be interpreted as a description of historical facts. It is a *theory* about how rational people *ought* to behave. The theory says it is rational for people to make some conservative decisions involving the surrender of certain individual rights in order to form a government that will, in turn, take care of them. The question is: Is it really so rational to do that? Even if we could trust the government not to operate in bad faith and abuse its power over those individuals, other problems arise. First, *people cannot surrender their conscience.* They cannot get out from under the moral obligation to think and decide what is right and wrong for themselves. The only rules a person should follow are those that the person agrees are morally justified. No appeal to a social contract, either explicit or implicit, can be made if it implies that the person has signed away his or her basic human rights or moral responsibilities. Second, *how can people form a contract which says that a government can morally do things that the individuals themselves cannot morally do?* If individuals are not justified in using force to redress their grievances or exact punishment, how is a government so justified? If individuals are not justified in coercing others, how is the government justified in such coercive policies as taxation?"

CRITIC: "Let me start again. The justification for having a government is to assure that the fundamental needs of each individual are met, that everyone's human rights are guaranteed, and that the safety and security of the community is maintained against threats from both internal and external forces. In an anarchistic society, no way exists to defend against vicious criminals and powerful invaders."

ADVOCATE: "But there are ways. People can form mutual protection societies; they can contract with private security agencies; they can band together in times of danger and work together to repel threats. But they do not have to form a government to do this. They do not have to vest a single group with the exclusive monopoly on the use of coercive force."

Areas for Further Inquiry

• Anarchists maintain that granting legitimacy to government implies two things: First, people who live in that community have the moral responsibility to obey the laws issued by the government of that state, and, second, only the government has the right to use coercive force to enforce laws or rules on that community. Do these two propositions follow from that idea?

• Advocates of anarchism disagree with everyone who defends the development of the state, whether they be democratic, socialistic, or totalitarian in their approach. Anarchists say that all other theories involve the common assumption that vesting some group with a monopoly over the use of coercive force is justified. If this assumption is correct—contrary to the anarchist's view—then how much power should that government have?

Philosophical Role Playing

Although generally it is more fun and more is learned when defending an unpopular philosophical position, this time take the critic's side first. The advocate of anarchism may have gone further than needed in the final comment of the debate. The advocate seems dangerously close to sanctioning the formation of a government, even a temporary one. In the role of critic, can you develop this idea further? As an advocate of anarchism, how would you reply?

In the role of the critic, respond to the two issues the anarchist raised in her second reply, namely the claims that (1) it's wrong to form a government because that means surrendering your moral conscience, and (2) it's wrong to form governments because they claim the right to do things that no individuals have the moral prerogative to do.

G-5 SOVEREIGNTY AND THE STATE

Question: Who ought to have ultimate authority in a community?

Conceptual tools: Sovereignty is the moral entitlement to exercise ultimate control in a state and, thereby, to secure the cooperation necessary to provide for the shared fundamental human needs of those who live in that state. If the entitlement extends to all aspects of life, it is considered complete. *If nothing the sovereign does can ever be challenged or questioned, then the authority is considered* absolute.

Individual Sovereignty

The *theory of individual sovereignty* maintains that each individual possesses the ultimate, absolute, and complete authority over herself or himself. (Individual sovereignty is the basis for the theory of anarchism; see G-4.) Forming a government implies vesting one group in a community with a monopoly on the exercise of coercive force. Anarchism asserts that there is no need for any government whatsoever. However, anarchists recognize the value of cooperation in meeting their fundamental shared human needs and the need to protect the community from threats that criminals or hostile outsiders pose. *Individual enforcement* of rights is the way many anarchists (who are not necessarily pacifists) would propose to meet these challenges.

An Argument for the Formation of a Government

The natural outgrowths of individual enforcement are mutual protection societies. Such societies, however, impose serious risks on others in a community. Specifically, mutual protection societies cannot guarantee reliable enforcement, due process, or the freedom from wrongful or unjust retaliation. Thus, individualistic enforcement produces a climate of general fear and apprehension, conditions that a community must take steps to change if it is to survive and flourish. So, the community forms a minimal or very limited government; that is, a single agency with the responsibility of prohibiting individual enforcement but also insuring the protection of *all* who live in that society. This government, by necessity, must be vested with the right to a monopoly over the use of coercive force.

Dictatorial Sovereignty

If I am not a sovereign individual, maybe somebody else is! The *theory of dictatorial sovereignty* maintains that some one person or subgroup in a society, but not everybody, has the moral entitlement to ultimate authority.

The sources of a person's right to claim *dictatorial sovereignty* is always a matter of serious debate. Some have asserted that God or another transcendental agency is the original source of their right to dictatorial sovereignty. The objection to this approach is our inability to verify such claims. A second approach is to assert dictatorial sovereignty simply because one has the military power to gain and hold control of the government. The objection here is that might does not make right—the power to rule and the moral authority to rule are two different things. A third strategy is to claim dictatorial sovereignty by virtue of one's specialized knowledge. It seems reasonable that a person with specialized expertise in a given area *ought* to be in charge of that area. But technical knowledge is not the same as wisdom or leadership. And verifying that one knows something is far easier than verifying that one is wise and worthy enough to be dictator.

Popular Sovereignty

If no individual or subgroup is sovereign, then maybe everyone, taken as a whole, is sovereign. The *theory of popular sovereignty* holds that *the people*, considered as a totality, hold the ultimate authority to demand cooperation of themselves in securing their shared fundamental human needs.

One serious objection to this theory is that the "will of the people" is nothing more than a theoretical fiction. No way exists to find out what "the people"—considered as a totality—really want. Elections tell us only about the opinion of a majority under the controlled circumstances of the particular issues that are put on the ballot to consider. Elections do not guarantee that everyone will abide by the results. Nor do elections guarantee that the result is moral or in the best interests of the people taken as a whole.

Areas for Further Inquiry

• If a society decides to no longer tolerate individualistic enforcement, is it reasonable that persons should at least be compensated for losses that might arise if they do not engage in individualistic enforcement? For example, if it is the government that legally prohibits and prevents you from retaliating against those who harm you or take property from you, should the government not compensate you for your losses? That is, what legal rights to compensation do the victims of crimes have, given that they have put their trust in the government to protect and defend them?

• Defenders of the argument for the formation of a government outlined above maintain that it morally justifies a *minimal government* because it does not advocate violating anyone's rights, nor does it assert that the government has any rights individuals do not have. Do you agree with this justification? What responses might an advocate of anarchism or individual sovereignty make? Can this argument be extended so as to justify government involvement in concerns such as education, health, environmental protection, transportation, communication, commerce, national defense, finance, welfare, agriculture, and international relations? Can the operation of government be funded without violating anyone's rights?

• Is it reasonable to accept dictatorial sovereignty in limited areas and nonabsolute ways? Suppose, for example, that experts were allowed to rule over specified areas of concern (e.g., the military, energy, the economy, public education, commerce, agriculture), but the experts could be kept in check by some higher authority whose rule is more complete and absolute. Could such a system work? Could it be morally justified? Would it necessarily involve violating any rights of individuals? Would it necessarily vest these experts (the government) with rights that no individuals have?

• Could popular sovereignty and individual sovereignty be combined? Suppose some domains of concern were designated to be under the control of the community as a whole (e.g., security, education, commerce, public safety), whereas all other areas not expressly put under the control of the government were left up to the individual to decide (e.g., recreation, entertainment, religion, sexuality). Could such a combination of conceptually incompatible theories work at the level of practical policy?

Philosophical Role Playing

Taking the role of an advocate of dictatorial sovereignty, define and defend the rights of government to interfere with the individual exercise of personal freedoms. For example, consider these two cases: (1) government control of school curriculum, such as forbidding the teaching of any given theory, e.g., creationism; (2) government control of sexual practices in order to protect society from the epidemic spread of a fatal disease. Consider the same two cases from the perspectives of individual sovereignty and popular sovereignty. Which approach seems most rational?

G-6 THE INDIVIDUAL AND THE STATE

Question: In terms of priorities, should the state serve the individual, or should the individual serve the state?

Fact: Inevitably in human society the interest of the one will conflict with the interest of the many.

An Argument for Classical Liberalism: The Individual Takes Priority

A fundamental goal for everyone is personal survival. Given survival, the other fundamental goals can be summed up as having the individual freedom to pursue one's own interests. To insure personal security and to protect themselves from one another and from outside threats, rational people form limited governments. Only behavior that causes or threatens to cause harm to another should be prohibited. Thus, the only legitimate purposes of government are to guarantee the security and individual freedoms of its citizens.

> *Classical liberalism* usually assumes *individual sovereignty* and an "eighteenth-century" view of human rights. (See G-4 and E-4.) It advocates maximizing *negative freedom* (described in F-5). By today's standards, classical liberals are on the political right and generally favor minimizing government interference.

Three Possible Objections to Classical Liberalism

First. A community is more than an atomistic collection of individuals. It is an organic whole. Nobody has proved that the good of each is the same as the good of the whole. But how can the common good be achieved without contradicting the principles of limited government?

Second. Cooperation to achieve shared purposes is more than an instrumental value. Cooperation is valuable in itself. Through cooperation, people find meaning in life and give purpose to their labor activity. But under classical liberalism, and its associated economic theory *capitalism*, each individual is put into competition with every other individual. Alienation, isolation, envy, corruption, and estrangement result as motives of petty self-interest prevail.

Third. Human rights go beyond leaving people alone to play whatever hand fate has dealt them. Human rights include an equal opportunity to participate in, enjoy, and contribute to society, including participating in government. They include the rights to own property, to work under safe conditions, to enjoy a decent standard of living including a secure retirement. They include an education, adequate medical care, welfare and material assistance in times of tragedy or catastrophe. But there is no provision under classical liberalism for government to insure all these rights.

An Argument for Fascism: The State Takes Priority

Survival and safety are important fundamental goals all individuals share. But the survival of the state, for its own sake and for the sake of present and future generations, is a more important goal. Pursuing the interests of the state keeps community spirit alive, preserves the traditions and values of a civilized society, and gives direction and meaning to the lives of individuals. Thus government ought to have the absolute and complete authority to pursue the fundamental goals of the state even if this overrides the safety and security of particular individuals.

> *Fascism* usually assumes *dictatorial sovereignty* (see G-5) and is *totalitarian* in form. That is, it claims total comprehensive authority over every social institution and facet of an individual's life that could possibly affect the long-term good of the state.

Three Possible Objections to Fascism

First. The reasons given for advancing the interests of the state may show that the state's interests are important, but they do not show that these interests should take *priority* over the interests of individuals.

Second. Cooperation may be a very valuable thing, but its value is enhanced if it is voluntary. Cooperation based on government tyranny is nothing more than extortion or slavery to the state. It is the antithesis of a dignified human existence.

Third. History has shown that it is exceptionally unwise to place one's trust in a totalitarian regime. The personal corruption that absolute power breeds; the well-known limitations of human knowledge and good will; the disasters of inadequate social planning and ineffective social control; and the horrors brought about by racism, prejudice, and stupidity all testify to the wisdom of dispersing and limiting government power.

An Argument for Socialism: Priority on Cooperation Toward Shared Goals

Survival, safety, health, education, dignified standards of living, and many other things are fundamental shared human goals. Many, if not all, of these basic fundamental human goals can best be achieved by planned cooperation in which the benefits and burdens of communal living are shared. Thus, the role of government is to plan and secure cooperation for the purpose of achieving the shared goals of individuals and the goals of the state.

> *Socialism* generally assumes *popular sovereignty* and takes a broader "twentieth-century" view of human rights. (See G-4

70

and E-4.) It advocates maximizing *positive freedom* (described in F-5). By today's standards, socialists are on the political left and generally favor expanding the role of government.

Three Possible Objections to Socialism

First.   As expressed above, voluntary cooperation is one thing, but forced cooperation is another. To the extent that the government forces cooperation, either directly by controlling a person's life and labor or indirectly through taxation and the redistribution of wealth, the value of cooperation is undermined if not destroyed.

Second.   As expressed above, the more power granted to government, the higher the risk of corruption, abuse, and costly error. It is better to let individuals pursue self-interest than to try to control everything.

Third.   Cooperation can be either *atomistic* or *organic.* That is, the good of the individuals can be pursued, or the good of the community as a totality can be pursued. Socialism, as presented here, does not indicate which should take priority if these come into conflict. Thus, our fundamental dilemma persists.

Capitalistic Socialism and Communistic Socialism

Politically, much is made of the difference between capitalism and communism. Capitalism, in its eighteenth-century *laissez faire* form, tends to be associated with classical liberalism. Communism, because of its twentieth-century manifestations, is often associated with totalitarianism. A look beyond the political rhetoric, however, at the actual policies being implemented reveals that both can be called socialistic. Granted, capitalism is more atomistic in that it gives special significance to individual liberties, whereas communism is more organic in that it emphasizes the value of society as a totality. Yet the policies of the capitalistic West include such things as social security, government regulation of commerce, Medicare, mandatory education of the young, government-insured banking, and a long list of other programs that go well beyond the limitations that classical liberalism would place on the role of government. It is interesting to review the writings of Karl Marx (1818–1883) and then realize how many of his proposals have actually been put into practice in "capitalistic" countries. Similarly, communist governments are realizing the need to use practice to temper theory. "Experiments" with competitive, free-enterprise economic programs, such as private farming, are showing that quality and productivity can be increased in ways that are inconsistent with traditional collectivist ideology.

Areas for Further Inquiry

• What parallels should be observed between the relationships of citizens to their governments and the relationships of business executives to the corporations that employ them? Internally which theory of government do corporations operate under? Which ought they to operate under?

Philosophical Role Playing

Defend each theory of government from the three possible objections presented. What additional arguments, pro and con, can you advance?

Neither classical liberalism, nor fascism, nor socialism is necessarily inconsistent with *democracy*, understood as the process of discovering the will of the people by means of voting. Yet each would place constraints on suffrage (who votes), on what issues can be voted about, and on the timing and structure of elections. Show how each theory could *democratize* itself in practice.

G-7   THE RULE OF LAW

Question: Why should there be laws, policies, and regulations?

Value judgment: The rule of law may be stern and unyielding, but it is better than the arbitrary and unpredictable rule of individual persons.

A Case Against the Rule of Law

Laws limit human freedom. Laws hinder spontaneity, creativity, and initiative. Laws can also be immoral, unfair, unwise, and repressive. In addition, laws are unnecessary because virtue comes from within. Social custom, morality, religion, and common sense give us enough guidance without adding laws. So, for all of the above reasons, it is better not to legislate.

A Case for the Rule of Law

First. Not all laws are negative. *Laws can open opportunities and create rights.* Laws also can clarify the conditions under which freedoms can be exercised without interference, e.g., civil rights legislation. Some laws also do limit freedom, e.g., traffic laws, but by limiting harmful and threatening behaviors, such laws can open up possibilities for people to do things more safely and successfully.

Second. Laws create social stability and order. They prevent individuals and government leaders from acting in arbitrary, prejudiced, unfair, and devious ways. By creating stability, they make possible the ordinary day-to-day commerce that makes society work: e.g., in employment practices; financial transactions; the regulation of education, health care, and transportation; and so on.

Third.   Morality and law are not one. Ethical principles are the measuring rods against which to evaluate laws. Human history has shown that when foolish or immoral laws have been enacted, people challenged them and refused to comply. The lives of Gandhi, Martin Luther King, Jr., Jesus, and others testify to the importance of not linking law and morality.

Fourth.   It would be nice if people were so good to each other that laws were superfluous, but many lack the virtues necessary to live in a civilized ethical society. Laws are necessary to regulate their behavior and *to protect people from the ruthless.*

Fifth.   As society becomes more complex and pluralistic, different customs, traditions, and religions not only fail to unify people, but they come into conflict with one another. Actions that exemplify common sense from one cultural perspective may be laughable from another. But laws *create the conditions for societies to be more complex,* and laws also can *protect the cultural richness* that a pluralistic society wishes to enjoy.

Unresolved Questions

A critic might object: "Granted advantages to the rule of law exist, but that doesn't answer the question of how far laws should go in regulating our lives. Assuming that less government is better than more, what is the *minimum* that must be put into legislation?

"Also, even laws that are not immoral can still be bad for other reasons. Some are ambiguous, overly specific, retroactive. Sometimes people do not know the laws. Sometimes the judicial process is biased, is infected with conflicts of interest, or fails to provide due process.

"And even if a community is blessed with wise laws, the laws could still fail to have the advantages described above. Enforcement might be arbitrary or selective; people might generally disregard the laws anyway; or enforcing one law might mean breaking others."

Minimum Prerequisites for the Rule of Law

Using the critic's observations, an advocate of the rule of law might respond by proposing minimal conditions that must be met for the rule of law to be successful.

At a *substantive* level—and assuming that less government is better than more—there must at least be laws that: (1) guarantee security from violence,

(2) guarantee access to the resources necessary to live, and (3) guarantee enforcement of contractual obligations.

At a *procedural* level, laws must: (1) apply generally rather than be targeted toward one specific person, (2) come into effect after they are legislated rather than being retroactive, (3) be relatively free from vagueness and ambiguity, (4) be promulgated by the proper authorities, (5) be generally accessible to the public, (6) be adjudicated in courts free from prejudice, bias, or conflict of interest, and (7) be adjudicated in ways that allow for due process and the opportunity to hear arguments regarding all sides of the issue at hand.

At a *practical* level: (1) enforcement must not be, or be seen as, arbitrary or selective; (2) enforcing one law must not imply breaking another; and (3) a community must generally follow its laws, making individual violations the exception rather than the common practice.

Areas for Further Inquiry

•   What other arguments can be advanced for or against the rule of law? Consider, for example, the argument that the laws are simply the tools used by the ruling class to maintain its power over others.

•   Are there other minimum *substantive, procedural, or practical* conditions for the rule of law that should be added? Is each one specified above necessary?

•   Granting that law limits freedom, how far should such limitations go? On what rational basis can specific limitations be justified?

Philosophical Role Playing

Marxists argue that morality and religion, like the law, are tools that the bourgeoisie uses to oppress the workers. The distinction between law and morality is merely conceptual since both have the same practical effect. Historically, laws were written with the idea that they did reflect the moral sentiments of the community. In the United States, many laws have a moral orientation that can be traced to the religious views of Puritan New Englanders. However, many Americans would maintain that there is, and should remain, a firm distinction between law and morality. Take the contrary view and argue in favor of legislating morality. As specific examples, consider abortion, smoking, prostitution, gambling, or drug abuse.

G-8   LAW AND INDIVIDUAL FREEDOM

Question: How can legal limitations on human freedom be justified?

Proposal: Legal restrictions are justified if they yield a net balance of freedom over limitations.

A Traditional Justification for Limiting Freedom

The less government the better. Each person has certain basic human rights and should be maximally free to exercise these rights. If everyone were absolutely free (able to act without legal restriction of any kind), then the fabric of society would be destroyed, and life in a complex, pluralistic community would be intolerable. Every person, no matter what the situation, should be treated equally and receive the same measure of a society's benefits and burdens. A state of affairs that involves a greater measure of freedom is better than another state of affairs that involves a lesser measure of freedom. Therefore, legal limitations on an individual's freedom are justified only if they are equally applied to all persons and also produce a net increase of freedom over restrictions.

A Debate over Limiting Freedom

A critic of the traditional view might object, "The case for limiting freedom assumes the theory of *classical liberalism*. But this theory has serious shortcomings. For one, it does not recognize a person's right to things that go beyond simply being left alone, things such as the right to an equal opportunity in employment, a basic education, decent health care, a decent standard of living, and so on." (See G-6.)

The advocate might respond, "Socialism and fascism, the other two theories of government, also have severe limitations. They err by granting government too much power. Is it better to be conservative and hold onto one's basic freedoms than to allow government to go unbridled?"

"Well, I have another concern," the critic might declare. "Your position assumes the thesis of egalitarianism, which also has serious limitations. For one, it violates the formal concept of justice by not attending to morally relevant differences and similarities." (See G-2.) "Also, your argument doesn't tell us what kind of freedom the laws should be trying to maximize."

"Let me clarify," the advocate might assert. "I advocate equal freedom under the law. This is called *formal freedom*. Any law that restricts some people and not others implies the creation of *privileges* and *immunities*. Such laws do not treat people as equals. The *first goal* of legislation should be to equalize formal freedom."

75

"I have a third concern," the critic might go on. "Your view assumes the theory of *social utility*, which has serious problems recognizing the intrinsic value of each individual and preserving individual rights in the face of desirable consequences that might come from compromising those rights." (See E-2.)

"You're right," the advocate might agree. "In terms of making social policy, the theory of social utility is an important tool. However, I grant your objection. Social utility should not be applied without regard for the intrinsic value of each person, nor should it override justice or any person's fundamental human rights."

"Thank you," the critic might say. "And I agree that *equalizing formal freedom is an important goal*. But it is not an absolute priority. Privileges and immunities are often justified. Only persons over a certain age have the privilege of voting. Law enforcement personnel who kill someone in the line of duty are immune from prosecution. Fire safety personnel who break and enter a burning building are also immune from prosecution. The issue is not how to do away with all privileges and immunities, but rather how to use them only when justifiable. A *second goal* of legal restrictions on freedom must be *preventing harm to persons and property*."

"It sounds like you're coming around to my point of view," the advocate might remark.

"Not really," the critic might come back. "I want to go further. Restricting everyone equally does not guarantee everyone an equal chance. *Effective freedom* is possessing the resources necessary to accomplish one's goals. A *third goal* of legislation should be to give everyone a fair and equal chance to become full and contributing members of society. This is done by legislation aimed at *equalizing and maximizing effective freedom* (e.g., welfare legislation, affirmative action laws, compulsory education, day care and school lunch programs, etc.).

"And one more thing," the critic might add, "there are sharks out there who take advantage of the others' ignorance. Fraud, swindles, shady deals, and the like victimize the old, the uneducated, the naive, and the trusting. Laws cannot fully protect people from their own bad judgment, but they should insure that people have truthful and relevant information so they can make a good decision. This implies a *fourth goal* of legislation: *maximizing the autonomy, especially the rationality, of individuals*." (See positive freedom in F-5.)

Areas for Further Inquiry

• Restrictive legislation is justified if it maximizes freedom, but which kinds of freedom: formal, effective, positive, negative, or all of these? If the answer is all, then in what order of priority?

• In a pluralistic society, different religions, customs, and mores often classify various behavior as offensive or immoral. Should laws exist to limit such behavior (e.g., the ritual sacrifice of pet animals during a cult religious service)? What if the behavior is not essentially harmful to anyone, but is simply offensive (e.g., public sexual contact between consenting adults)? What if some are convinced the practice is harmful, but others are convinced it is not (e.g., smoking, distributing pornography, abortion)? What if some see positive social good coming from a practice, but others see it as intrinsically immoral (e.g., legalizing certain drugs or conducting biomedical experiments on animals)?

Philosophical Role Playing

The debate above ended with considerable agreement, and four goals that justify legal restrictions on freedom were identified. But in the process, the socialistic and fascistic perspectives were passed over rather quickly. Also restrictions were mentioned that prevented the pure application of the theory of social utility. Consider the issue of legal restrictions on various kinds of freedom once again, but this time play the role of a socialist and then a fascist in articulating the goals that justify such limits. Then, playing the role of a pure utilitarian (see E-2) who has no concern for values such as respect for persons or justice unless these make sense in terms of social utility, reconsider your original answers to the questions in the "Areas for Further Inquiry" section.

If you were a member of the state legislature, what would your position be on these bills: A bill to require protective helmets of all motorcycle riders, a bill to legalize prostitution, a bill to prohibit X-rated movies from cable TV, a bill requiring annual AIDS testing of all persons aged eighteen to forty, a bill restricting the press's access to information regarding the trials of persons accused of treason, a bill granting full rights of citizenship only to the first natural-born children in a family, a bill requiring mandatory sterilization of any person found guilty of a felony sex offense, a bill legalizing the sale of steroids to minors.

KNOWLEDGE

K-1   DOGMATIC SKEPTICISM

Question: Can I know anything for certain?
Analysis: Knowledge means true, justified belief.

A Classical Argument for Skepticism

A person, X, can claim to know a proposition, *p*, if—and only if—(1) *p* is true, (2) X believes that *p* is true, and (3) X is *fully justified* in believing that *p* is true. X is fully justified in believing *p* if, and only if, there is *no possibility* of X having reason to doubt *p* is true. People claim to know things about religion, morality, art, other people (including what they are thinking or why they are behaving in certain ways), the physical world (including what causes things to happen), history, abstract concepts such as the laws of mathematics, their own feelings, their own ideas, and their own perceptions. All the things people claim to know come either from their own sense perceptions or the ideas in their own mind. (E.g., we perceive physical objects, and we remember our own past.) Both sense perceptions and our own ideas are untrustworthy. So, certainty is impossible; we cannot know anything.

From Skepticism to Solipsism

A critic might inquire, "How far do you plan to take this? Questioning knowledge in the areas of art, ethics, and religion is not new. But surely skepticism is not going to challenge science or common sense!"

"That's a timid mistake," the advocate of skepticism might reply. "I must follow the argument wherever its logic leads. *Dogmatic skepticism* is the position that *nothing* can be known for certain. This means I cannot know that normative statements, historical or religious claims, or statements about physical or social reality are correct. I cannot know that what my senses tell me has anything to do with how the world really is. I cannot know that other persons exist or that any mind is in existence except my own."

> The philosophical position which maintains that there is no other mind in existence except one's own is known as *solipsism.*

The Argument from Illusion

The heart of the classical argument for skepticism is its defense of the claim that we cannot trust either our sense perceptions or our own ideas. A critic of this view might challenge it by saying, "I feel the chair beneath me; I see the coins and other objects on my desk; I remember I have an appointment at noon. How can I be mistaken about these things?"

To this, a person defending skepticism, as did Descartes (1596–1650), might respond, "We have all experienced being deceived by other people, being misled by our senses, remembering things incorrectly and the like. But the unreliability of our senses and our memories goes beyond these common kinds of cases. Consider, for example, *sensory illusions* or hallucinations. Even beyond this, our ideas might not be accurate. Imagine, for example, that you are *dreaming* or under the influence of some subtle but powerful mind-altering drug. Or maybe you are being systematically deceived for malicious reasons by a powerful force (an *evil genius*) who is capable of weaving a web of *illusion so well that it can never be detected.* This illusion is so complete that even your feelings, your mental concepts, and your memories are being tampered with. All these possibilities create *doubts* about the reliability of our senses and our ideas as sources of accurate information and certainty.

I Think, So I Exist

CRITIC: "Your skeptical argument concerning illusion is impressive. But it only proves to me that maybe *what* I see is not as I see it. The argument does not prove that I am not having the experience of seeing. In other words, I may not be sure about the existence and nature of physical objects, but I am sure that I am experiencing sensory phenomena. I know what it feels like to sit down; I hear a high-pitched whine; I see a swatch of yellow and a splash of blue. I am certain about these facts! And more, the fact of my having any experiences at all proves that I exist. This is certain: I think, therefore I exist. *Cogito ergo sum.*"

79

SKEPTIC: "The idea that I am a mind that thinks does not follow from having one or more thoughts. Supposing that there is an *I* having these thoughts makes assumptions about the *continuity of awareness* and *personal identity* that cannot be verified. I have more to say about your other comments concerning having experiences: My remarks appear in the criticisms of *epistemological phenomenalism*." (See K-2.)

Other Minds

CRITIC: "I don't know why you are talking to me. Your behavior is self-defeating. How can you argue with me about the merits of skepticism if you think that I am not real? Do you draw comfort from others who share your views? What is it like to call a meeting of solipsists? Does anybody show up? How do you know? Look, let's stop the silly pretending. We both know other persons exist. We can see how they behave and how they react to situations. We know when we hear laughter that another human mind resides inside that laughing body. We know when we see someone wince and clutch a cut arm that someone is experiencing pain. Other minds, beside one's own, exist, my friend."

SKEPTIC: "I'm tempted not to answer at all, but that would be as mistaken as your objection. You see, the burden of proof is on you, not me. All I have to maintain is that I cannot *know for certain* that other minds exist. There's nothing absurd about disputing the merits of skepticism if one is *not sure* whether there are other conscious, thinking beings. I'm saying only that I cannot be certain there are such beings, not that I know there are none. But you will have a chance to defend your feeble arguments from my criticisms when we get to the issue of the existence of other minds." (See K-3.)

Knowledge and Illusion

CRITIC: "Your analysis of knowledge is demonstrably mistaken. Knowing does not imply certitude. We can say we know something even if we are mistaken. And you use the word *illusion* incorrectly, too. This is what leads to all the trouble. To say that something is an illusion means that it is a trick that can, in principle, be discovered and explained. There can be no illusion that is so systematic as to be entirely and always undetectable. Your entire argument is a conceptual confusion. I don't know why I'm trying to refute it. I should simply disregard it. And if that isn't obvious enough, I should know that any argument which ends up in solipsism must have a false premise or false assumption operating someplace. Solipsism is absurd."

SKEPTIC: "Now don't get testy. I know your frustrations. Remember, I'm no more happy being a skeptic than you would be. But, as I said, I must follow where logic leads. As to your last-ditch efforts, if people ordinarily use the word *know* in ways that do not imply certitude, they are just being sloppy. In any case, the issue is not knowledge but whether *certainty* is possible. As to your comments about my use of the word *illusion,* in order to show that my entire argument is a conceptual confusion you must do more than point out how I might be misusing a single word. Finally, regarding solipsism, the view is not self-contradictory, even if it is contrary to intuition. But if you wish to insist that my skepticism is based on a false assumption or false premise, please point it out."

Areas for Further Inquiry

• Skepticism reduces knowing why, knowing how, knowing when, knowing whether, and so on, to *propositional knowledge* or *knowing that.* It sees advantage in the idea that the proposition in question must be either true or false. Are there other kinds of knowledge beside propositional knowledge? If so, how do they relate to *knowing that?*

• Knowledge has been defined as *true, justified belief.* Perhaps that definition is too strong. What if knowledge were defined as *warranted assertability*—meaning that a person could claim to *know* something if the person could assert it as true on the basis of the appropriate evidence and when no basis for *reasonable* doubt regarding that assertion existed? Would the arguments of skepticism still prevail using this *weaker* definition of knowledge? Is the definition, on its own merits, acceptable?

• Considering the importance of the *argument from illusion* to the skeptic's position, do you think that more should be said in reply to the critic's claim that the skeptic is confused about what illusions really are? Could skepticism be defended without appeal to this argument?

Philosophical Role Playing

Defend skepticism. Or if that is too easy, refute it.

K-2   KNOWLEDGE OF PHYSICAL OBJECTS

Question: How can one refute the skeptic's arguments regarding the impossibility of knowing physical objects?

Assumption: Statements about the phenomena immediately present to one's senses are incorrigible; that is, immune from revision by the introduction of other evidence.

81

A First Try at Refuting the Skeptic

The skeptic is correct in saying our senses can mislead us regarding the true character of physical objects. (For example, that coin on my desk looks elliptical from this angle, but it is really flat and circular.) Although the object does not change, as I look at an object while changing my perspective, there is no interruption in my experience of its continuously changing appearance. So, in perception we experience only sense data. A person's statements about the sense data presently available to that person's senses are incorrigible. Thus, a statement about a physical object is equivalent to a set of statements about the availability of potential sense data to a normal observer from a given perspective under standard conditions. Therefore—contrary to the skeptic—from knowledge of sense data one can validly reason to knowledge about physical objects.

> *Phenomenalism* is the theory that the only things a person really perceives are sense data or that statements about physical objects are equivalent to groups of statements about sense data.

A Skeptic's Objections

SKEPTIC: "There are two reasons to reject your assumption that statements about physical objects are equivalent to sets of statements about available sense data. First, the number of possible ways to experience an object is indefinitely large. No *complete* analysis of statements about physical objects in terms of sets of statements about sense data has ever been given. It is doubtful that a complete analysis can ever be given. Second, physical objects are *public*, but sense data are private. How can statements about private sense data be equivalent to a statement about a public physical object?

"But if we can't make a complete or equivalent analysis of physical object statements in terms of sense data statements, then your inferences to knowledge about physical objects from knowledge of sense data will not be valid (even though they may be highly warranted). And, as a result, certainty will have escaped you.

"Another problem I have is with the idea that sense data claims are incorrigible. You mentioned a *normal* observer under *standard* conditions. This implies that nonnormal and nonstandard cases exist. So, if someone claims to know something because of statements about sense data, that knowledge claim may be subject to revision. It is not incorrigible.

"Also, I'm not sure I agree that sense data claims are private. 'Through the dirty windshield of my car the sky looks smoggy purple,' is public; it is something that another person can verify. And the statement presumes a certain set of viewing conditions. For example, 'that's true, but only if you are driving north through Los Angeles in the late afternoon and there are no clouds,' a passenger in my car might say.

"Finally, an important thing about physical objects is that they exist through time independent of anyone's sense data. (Intelligent life is out there someplace, but nobody from earth has yet made contact.) Your argument has not adequately accounted for the continuity of physical objects, the relative constancy of their properties, and their existence in situations in which they cannot be perceived."

A Second Try at Refuting the Skeptic

No reason exists to suppose that what we experience during hallucinations and illusions is connected with physical objects since these experiences can be explained in terms of alterations in the condition of the observer (e.g., experiences under the influence of drugs, in times of high stress, or influenced by strong personal bias) or in the environment (e.g., insufficient light or too much background noise). Saying that things can appear other than the way they are need not imply that their appearances are necessarily misleading. (For example, that coin on my desk is circular, but it can, and does, appear elliptical when seen from this angle.) Statements about one's experience are open to revision, but they can still be relied on as a basis for knowledge claims provided no reason exists to doubt them. Reliable knowledge claims regarding physical objects can be the result of justified or warranted inferences, in contrast to valid inferences (see L-3), from statements about one's experiences. Therefore, knowledge about physical objects can be inferred from knowledge about our experience of those objects.

The Skeptic's Second Turn

SKEPTIC: "I see you've lowered your standard of knowledge. But by settling for *warranted assertability*, my demand for guarantees of *certainty* are not met. Only logically valid arguments can insure that the conclusion *must* be true if the premises are all true. Worse, if I were to accept your conclusion, I would find myself in the awkward position of saying things as silly sounding as: 'I *know* this assertion *about the world is true* because it is warranted, *but it's really false.*' You had better reconsider your analysis of knowing. Knowing that *p* implies that *p* is true.

"As to other aspects of your argument, exactly what are the *ideal* environmental conditions? Exactly what makes an observer *normal*? Key concepts in your argument are much too vague.

"Finally, your argument has not explained what conditions cause physical objects to be experienced in the ways we experience them. As a result, it has not provided a basis to guide the formulation and testing of scientific inferences from premises expressing our experiences to conclusions regarding the exact nature of physical objects."

Areas for Further Inquiry

Suppose that in the final analysis both arguments fail to refute the skeptic regarding the possibility of obtaining knowledge of physical objects from sense perceptions. What third approach might salvage the common sense idea that we can and do know things about the world around us?

Philosophical Role Playing

If this were tennis, "advantage skeptic," at least so far. But if anything is certain, it is that neither debate is over yet. How would you defend, repair, or restate both arguments in response to the criticisms the skeptic presented?

K-3 KNOWLEDGE OF OTHER MINDS

Question: How can one refute solipsism?

Problem: Although the skeptic's argument—that I cannot be certain that any other mind beside my own exists—seems powerful, it is not persuasive. Something must be wrong with it someplace, if only I could find it.

An Argument from Analogy for the Existence of Other Minds

Observing my own behavior and that of other people, I note that their behavior is similar to my own in many ways. I have thoughts, emotions, reactions, and ideas that cause me to behave the way I do—in short, I have a mind. The causes of the others' behaviors are similar to the causes of my own behaviors. Therefore, I have a mind, and, by analogy, they have minds too.

A Debate over the Argument

SKEPTIC: "What is your evidence for thinking that the behavior of other people is similar to your own?"

ADVOCATE: "I have advanced the argument from analogy for the existence of other minds in different ways at different times, so my evidence varies from one version to another. Here is some of the evidence: Certain behaviors are commonly associated with certain mental states, for example, things people do when they are angry, happy, in pain, depressed, relaxed, stressed, grieving, and so on. When I see others doing those behaviors, I can infer, by analogy, that they are experiencing particular mental states because when I do those things, I am experiencing those mental states. But at times I focus on analyzing the use of language. People say things in certain circumstances. They say what I would say if I were having such and such thoughts. So, they are probably having analogous thoughts. Or if we think of each word in a language as possessing a meaning, then when I successfully communicate in words with someone else, I am conveying the meaning of each word from my mind to another person's mind using the vehicle of language."

SKEPTIC: "Look again at the theory of word meaning you assume in your response. Human communication depends on conventions and intentions, not just reference. But apart from this, your argument seems to presume a kind of causal interaction between the mind and the body it inhabits. How does the mind, which might be assumed to be spiritual, *cause* the body, which is physical, to behave?"

ADVOCATE: "Specifying the interactive relationship between the mind and the body is difficult. (See N-1 and N-4.) Whatever the relationship is in my case, I assume it is the same in the case of other people."

SKEPTIC: "You know, your argument is only an analogy, and a weak one at that. (See L-4.) You only examine one case—my assertion that my behavior is associated with mental states. Such an argument can support its conclusion with only a weak inductive warrant, not the deductive validity we skeptics demand. Another problem with your particular analogy is that it can never be verified. It assumes that *the minds of others are inaccessible.* I cannot know another's thoughts and feelings; I can only infer what they probably are from what I observe.

"Indeed, I think your argument is so weak that you might as well argue that when you observe the behavior of others you never experience the presence of any thoughts or feelings except your own. Thus, others are robots or automatons, and yours is the only mind in existence."

ADVOCATE: "That would make me a solipsist!"

A Second Try: Focus on Behavior Only

Minds do not lurk inaccessibly behind behaviors; mental states are nothing but sets of behaviors. *Phenomenalism* (see K-2) or some comparable theory that knowledge of physical objects is possible is true. Therefore, claims of knowledge of other minds are as valid as any other knowledge claims about the physical observable world.

> *Philosophical behaviorism* is a theory which claims that statements about mental states can be reduced to statements about sets of behaviors. See also N-2.

A Skeptic's Rebuttal

SKEPTIC: "I would like to be nice about it, but asking me to forget the objections I made earlier (see K-2) and to agree to some form of *phenomenalism* is too much. Besides, I'm having trouble with your first claim. As a description of reality, it is false. Not all behaviors accurately reveal a person's mental state. Pretending, play acting, and deliberate deception, for example, do not. But, as a stipulation, it is a distortion of language. As a result, my friend, your argument fails."

A Third Try: Looking at Ordinary Language

Ordinarily speaking, when we make statements such as, "I enjoy biking," we do not call them *observations* or *reports* or *descriptions* resulting from an *inspection of our interior mental states*, but rather they are *authoritative acts of self-definition*. Ordinarily, when someone says he has a pain in his calf muscle, it is reasonable to ask if it is dull, sharp, superficial, deep, and so on, and having "felt the same pain," we know what he means. First person statements about present feelings or emotional states are not ordinarily private, hidden, and incorrigible revelations; they are publicly verifiable expressions. (Did you ever see someone who was really angry scream, "I'm not angry!" in absolute frustration?) Commonly the words we use to ascribe mental states to ourselves are used in precisely the same way when we ascribe mental states to others. (E.g., "You and I felt the same way about that, we hated it," does not imply two meanings of *felt* or *hate*.) So, judging from how we ordinarily talk about such things, the feelings, attitudes, emotions, and thoughts of others are not inaccessible; rather they are just as open to public examination as my own are. Therefore, I can make warranted assertions about other minds with varying degrees of awareness, understanding, empathy, and certainty.

A Skeptic's Reply

SKEPTIC: "The ordinary language approach relies *uncritically* on how people happen to talk. What if we ordinarily said things like, "She lied because she is a witch." Would that make her a witch? No. Then neither does an uncritical, unreflective appeal to ordinary talk solve any philosophical problems. In addition—and I'm sure I've already mentioned this—*warranted assertability* is not validity, and it's also not absolute certainty. Let's keep sight of our goals."

Areas for Further Inquiry

Those who look to ordinary language for clues about philosophical puzzles claim they are not trying to "solve" problems but to "dissolve" them. They claim that philosophical problems arise because of faulty assumptions about how words are used, which, once revealed, lose their power to mislead us. How could this approach be used to respond to the dogmatic skepticism of K-1?

Philosophical Role Playing

Here, too, the skeptic seems to have the upper hand. But much more sophistication can be achieved in all three approaches. Try to defend each from the objections the skeptic raised.

K-4   REASON AND EXPERIENCE

Question: How do we know that various kinds of statements are true?

Insight: Perhaps we can only know the truth or falsity of some statements on the basis of empirical investigation whereas for other statements, reasoning regarding the concepts involved is all we require.

Truths of Reason and Truths of Experience

Consider these statements and ask yourself if each is true or false. If you are not sure, ask yourself how you might find out.

1. The petals of the Peace rose blossoms are yellow with tinges of pink.
2. Bats find their way in the dark with the aid of a kind of sonar.
3. Prairie falcons nest alongside hawks in southwestern Wyoming.
4. Mrs. Angela Perkowski is the president of the United States.
5. One way AIDS is transmitted is sexually via a retrovirus.

How might people know whether each of the above is true or false? The answer, in general terms, is that we know these kinds of things on the basis of experience, either firsthand or indirectly from the research and observations of others. For now, let's call these kinds of statements *truths of experience.*

By contrast, consider these statements, and ask yourself if each is true or false. If you are not sure, how might you find out?

6. Space is a three-dimensional construct.
7. If A contains B, and B contains C, then A contains C.
8. Everyone who has a sister has a sibling.
9. Every effect has a cause.
10. In base ten, two plus seven equals nine.

In general terms, we can say that people know that each of the above is true on the basis of knowing what the ideas (concepts, words) involved mean. For now let's call these kinds of statements *truths of reason.*

The Analytic/Synthetic Distinction

A controversy lasting centuries has surrounded the distinction between truths of reason and truths of experience. Not the least of the difficulties involves how to give a more technical definition of each kind! Should we, for example, say that the truths of reason are *analytic,* meaning they are true (or false) strictly on the basis of meanings of the words involved? For example, "I know a married bachelor" would be analytically false because, given the meanings of the words *married* and *bachelor,* there couldn't be anyone who fits that description. By contrast, "I know someone who is married" is not analytic; I can't tell if it is true or false just by correctly understanding it. This example would be classified as a *synthetic* statement.

Those who advocate the "analytic/synthetic" distinction generally maintain that the two classes of statements are mutually exclusive. So, we can define a "synthetic statement" as any statement that is not analytic. This begs the key questions: How well does the analytic/synthetic distinction fit the truths of reason/truths of experience distinction?

The A Priori/Empirical Distinction

A more traditional way to approach the difference between truths of reason and truths of experience is by investigating how statements of each kind can be philosophically justified. It is argued that the *only* way to know truths of experience is for some person actually to conduct an empirical investigation and discover the truth. By contrast, it is argued that the *only* way to justify a truth of reason is through achieving a proper understanding of the relationships of the ideas involved. For this, and other historical reasons, those we have called "truths of experience" are known as *empirical statements,* and those we have called "truths of reason" are known as *a priori statements.*

One problem with this approach is that we can often find troublesome examples that make the a priori/empirical distinction appear culturally or historically relative if not question begging. For example, how should these cases be classified?

11. The world is flat. (Said in Madrid in 1450.)

12. Through a point outside a line, one and only one straight line can be drawn that is parallel to the given line.

13. Socrates, being bald, has no hair.

The Vital Importance of the Difference

For many philosophers in earlier centuries, the importance of carefully describing the difference between truths of reason and truths of experience had little to do with their views about language or logic. The real issues were epistemological and metaphysical. If two very different kinds of truths existed, then there would have to be two very different ways in which we could know the truth. Human experience could yield knowledge of only the *empirical* truths. But everything worth knowing was an a priori truth of metaphysics, morality, and religion. Knowledge of these a priori truths obviously did not come through the misleading vehicle of human experience. Hence, it was vital that there be a legitimate alternative *source* of truth, namely reason, with which to achieve knowledge not weakened by the uncertainties and changing facts of *empirical* experience.

Ironically, in recent times the distinction has retained its importance but has advanced an opposite agenda. To differentiate the soft-minded myths and superstitions of metaphysics, morality, and religion from the tough-minded effort of digging out the facts as they really are, it became important to emphasize the radical difference between what we can know (namely *empirical* statements) from all the nonsense (namely any of those so-called truths of reason that traditional philosophers called a priori and that were not true or false strictly on the basis of what their words meant, that is, *analytic statements*).

A Difference in Degree, Not Kind

Imagine the consternation created by the idea that the difference between the truths of reason and truths of experience is only a matter of degrees. It is not a difference of kinds or sources of truth. According to this interpretation, because some are more central to our lives and closer to the heart of our world views whereas others are philosophically peripheral, we would sooner discard some beliefs than others. "Oh, so Socrates isn't bald. Fine. No problem." Statements like 11, even though false, died hard. And 12, thought to be central to geometry for centuries, was even tougher to discard. On the other extreme, our level of commitment to 9 and 10 is thought to be virtually absolute. (More is said about how theories are built and how world views are evaluated in T-1 and T-3.)

Sources and Kinds of Truth

In philosophy a *rationalist* is anyone who holds the view that reason can be a source and justification of truth. The continental rationalists, chiefly Descartes (1596–1650), Spinoza (1632–1677) and Leibniz (1646–1716), tended to give great prominence to a priori statements in the development of their philosophical views. They often maintained what has come to be known as the *coherence theory of truth.* Using this theory of truth, one would include in one's set of beliefs only those statements that were not inconsistent with each other and not inconsistent with one's fundamental, well-justified (on the basis of reason) first principles. The broader one's coherent set of beliefs, the better one's philosophical "system of thought" is said to be.

In philosophy an *empiricist* is anyone who holds the view that experience can be a source and justification of truth. The British empiricists, chiefly Hume (1711–1776), Locke (1632–1704) and Berkeley (1685–1783), tended to give major prominence to *empirical* statements and methods in the development of their philosophical positions. They tended to operate on what has come to be known as the *correspondence theory of truth.* Using this theory of truth, one would include in one's set of beliefs only those statements whose content "correspond-ed" with the facts of reality. The more individual truths it contains about reality, the better one's intellectual "body of knowledge" is thought to be.

Areas for Further Inquiry

• Are all empirical statements synthetic and all a priori statements analytic? Can you think of any counterexamples?

• Another key distinction, along with the empirical/a priori distinction, that bolsters twentieth-century empiricists is the fact/value distinction. According to this, a sharp difference exists between statements that express facts and those that express value judgments. Can you find any counterexamples to that view? (Suggestion: See M-3.)

Philosophical Role Playing

Defend the view that the difference between the truths of reason and the truths of experience is a matter of degrees, not kind.

K-5   NONHUMAN INTELLIGENCE

Question: Other than in the human species, does artificial or natural intelligence exist on this planet?

Observation: The human species is extremely egotistical in presuming it alone possesses consciousness and hence is entitled to treat all other living and mechanical things as mere tools to satisfy its own needs.

A Case for Artificial Intelligence

First consideration. Look at what computers can do. They can solve mathematical problems at incredible speed. They can recognize shapes, colors, and motion. They can compose music, play chess, recognize odors, receive input and produce output in several languages; and, in conjunction with robotics, they can interact with the environment.

Second consideration.   Research on expert systems by knowledge engineers has led to programs that can exactly reproduce the decision-making procedures and problem-solving strategies of persons who are experts in specific fields. Such programs are already in use, and better ones are constantly being developed. These programs are composed of the same two things that define human expertise, an *inference engine* and *an information base.*

Third consideration.   Research on parallel processing, goal-oriented decision procedures, inductive inference techniques, natural language processing, and machine learning (where computers reprogram themselves on the basis of self-evaluations of their own performance) shows that genuine artificial intelligence is achievable.

Fourth consideration.   Suppose you put a computer and a person in a room, and you communicate in writing with both of them, simulating all aspects of human intelligence. If in the end you cannot tell the difference between interacting with the computer or the person, then—except for bias— there is no operational reason why you cannot ascribe intelligence to the computer. (This identification procedure is called a *Turing test* after the logician and computer pioneer Alan Turing [1912–1954].)

Conclusion.   So, the only thing standing in the way of acknowledging artificial intelligence as the equivalent of human intelligence is prejudice. Machines *understand* things, and the computer program *explains* what human understanding really means.

A Case Against Artificial Intelligence

First consideration.   When we talk about human intelligence, we are specifically interested in *intentionality,* or the capabilities of *believing, intending, desiring, hoping,* and so on that are *directed toward* specific objects or states of affairs. (For example, I intend to be home on time for dinner. I believe I could have done a better job of explaining my intentions to her.) Even if machines can simulate the interactions and replicate the output, this does not prove that they have *intentional states* (believing, intending, desiring, comprehending, understanding, and so forth).

Second consideration.   Another aspect of human intelligence is emotional and perceptual. We are capable of love, hate, fear, passion, compulsion, anxiety, grief, joy, elation, enthusiasm. We can feel pain and pleasure. No

91

matter how much a computer prints out sentences expressing those feelings, it cannot *feel* those emotions or *experience* those sensations.

Third consideration.   Imagine I am put in a room and given several pages of text in a foreign language, one I do not understand at all. Now suppose I am also given some rules, written in my native language, to help me figure out which shapes and squiggles of the foreign language to draw and hand out of the room based on which shapes and squiggles are first handed in to me. If I become skilled at picking out the right shapes and passing them out of the room, I might be able to fool a native speaker of that other language into thinking that I *understood* that language. But the truth is that I have no clue as to what questions are being asked of me nor what my answers could possibly mean. Machines are no different. (This kind of response is called the *Chinese room* argument.)

Conclusion.   So long as machines function at the purely formal level—that is, by operating only on the level of the shapes, structures, or syntax of a language, but never operating at the level of semantics, language, meaning, and intentionality—they cannot be said to *understand* what they are doing no matter how amazingly fast or accurate their output is.

For Artificial Intelligence

ADVOCATE: "Regarding intentionality, whatever the causal processes involved, sooner or later we will be able to duplicate them artificially. Of that I'm confident.

"Also, consider the difference between *understanding* a native language and *understanding* a second language. When I first start learning a second language, I take in sounds and written expressions, correlate them with elements in my native language, and then output them in the second language. But when do I *understand* the second language? You critics of artificial intelligence are imposing a concept of understanding that is too occult to be helpful."

Against Artificial Intelligence

CRITIC: "If intentionality could be duplicated artificially, as you have suggested, then there is no problem with calling that machine intelligent. But the original argument was whether machines that operated by computational processes over purely formal or syntactic elements were intelligent. Such machines are not.

"Besides, I agree that *intelligent machines* already exist! They operate biochemically, and we call them *brains*. Humans have such machines. There is no reason to suppose that talking about consciousness implies talking about some spiritual substance other than the brain (such as a soul). Mental states *are* intrinsically connected to what happens in the brain.

"But, if you think machines are intelligent in exactly the same way as humans are, then how do you morally justify turning machines off?"

The Corollary: Animal Intelligence and Animal Rights

ADVOCATE: "If the human mind and human intelligence are strictly brain related and not dependent on some transcendental or spiritual principle such as the soul, then we should expect to find *genuine intelligence* in other large-brained animals, such as dolphins and chimpanzees. Indeed, research has shown that other species of animals are capable of language acquisition, complex social interaction, tool making, and the transmission of acquired skills and information between individuals. Hence, animals have genuine intelligence. And if intelligence is the basis for ascribing basic natural rights to humans, then animals have rights too."

Areas for Further Inquiry

The points sketched above only begin to identify and address some of the epistemological, metaphysical, and moral issues involved in the possibility of artificial or animal intelligence. What is your considered opinion on the possibility of nonhuman intelligence and its moral implications?

Philosophical Role Playing

Design and defend a policy entitled the "Rights of Intelligent Entities" that would apply equally to intelligent humans, intelligent animals, and intelligent machines.

LOGIC

L-1   ASSUMPTIONS

Question: What are assumptions and how do they work in arguments?

Warning: Not everything the author of an argument assumes turns out true.

Logic and Proving Things True

Logic is the branch of philosophy that studies the relationships between the premises and conclusions of arguments and emphasizes finding objective criteria for assessing the logical quality of different kinds of arguments. In P-4, "Giving Reasons," I defined an *argument* as a *set of statements,* one of which, called the *conclusion,* the author of the argument is trying to demonstrate to be true; the other(s) of which, called the *premise(s),* the author of the argument offers as grounds for accepting the conclusion. In making an argument, an author is trying to *prove* something; namely, that the claim presented as the conclusion of the argument is true. Thus, one important goal of logic is to help us better evaluate how successful the author's argument actually is.

Focusing on the product of the author's efforts, we can define a *proof* as an argument an author offers in support of a point of view. There are many examples of proofs in this book, often located in paragraphs headed "An Argument for . . ." In the sections on "Ethics," "Freedom," "Knowledge," "Nature," and "Religion," these are plentiful. As you can see from reading the debates and criticisms that follow those proofs, *proof* does *not* necessarily mean a *successful* demonstration; that remains an open question. To evaluate a proof,

94

apply the steps given in P-4: Find the proof, rewrite it, and then assess it. Assessment involves two tests: the test for how logically strong the argument is and the test for whether the premises are in fact true. *Logic* focuses on the first test, namely how strong the inferential relationship is between the premises of the argument and the claim the author is trying to establish.

Assumptions of Proofs and Claims

Ordinarily the person offering a proof presumes that its premises are sufficiently obvious and its inferences sufficiently intuitive that the proof will be accepted as a sound demonstration of the truth of her desired conclusion. However, as you can see from reading the criticisms of proofs offered in other sections of this book, authors are not always right. "Sufficiently obvious" and "sufficiently intuitive" are relative to the intended audience. What is obvious to a team of research scientists might be obscure to a group of poets and vice versa. Proofs, in other words, are tools of demonstration people use in a given context. To uncritically isolate the proof from its context can lead to problems, particularly regarding how really obvious the author's premises are.

Any premise can be presented in a given context as an assumption or not as an assumption. If the author offers an independent argument in support of a premise, then that premise is not an assumption; otherwise it is. To understand this use of the word *assumption*, remember that the ordinary idea of an assumption is a statement that is *taken for granted* in a given context of discussion. In other words, assumptions are statements that are taken to be more or less obviously true and not in need of independent justification and defense in a given context of discussion. The premises a person's argument depends on may or may not be assumptions, understood in this sense. If the author thinks a given premise might not be obvious, he will often provide a separate argument in support of that premise. But at times a premise might be so obvious in a given context that actually speaking it would be redundant or sound silly. For example, "Socrates is human. So, he's mortal," omits the premise "All humans are mortal." Unspoken premises can almost always be classified as assumptions because authors seldom provide a backup demonstration to support them.

People can also make assumptions when they present *claims*. A *claim* is an assertion expressing a point of view. The purpose of a proof is to demonstrate a claim. But at times people just make claims without trying to prove they are true, as, for example, in simply expressing an opinion: "The Tigers are the best team in baseball today." To which claim, someone might respond, "What makes you assume that?" or "What reason is there to think that?" or "Prove it!"

Digging Out Unspoken Assumptions

Identifying and evaluating a person's unspoken (implicit) assumptions is central to critically assessing the quality of a person's arguments and to deciding whether or not to accept a person's claims as true. In the sections of this text where proofs are presented and criticized, the discussion often includes a challenge based on the idea that the original argument depended on one or more unstated assumptions. In G-8, "Law and Individual Freedom," for example, the debate following the initial argument has the critic pointing out three hefty but unspoken assumptions the original author made.

Often when brought to light and examined, unspoken assumptions turn out to be false—thus making the arguments that depend on them unacceptable. The best way to identify assumptions is to probe claims and arguments looking for the *reasons why*. Ask: Why do you think that claim is true? Why do you think this premise is true? What reasons might there be for accepting that claim or believing this premise? In effect, to *uncover* assumptions is to get behind a person's claims and arguments and figure out what the person takes as the basis for his or her assertions.

Not every assumption is false. Nor is it an error to make assumptions. It might be argued, in fact, that we cannot get along without making some assumptions. But be cautious: *Much of the progress in philosophy as well as in other areas of life is achieved by unearthing the false or questionable assumptions lurking behind someone's apparently obvious assertions.*

The Strategy of Reduction to Absurdity

When trying to demonstrate the truth of a statement, assuming the statement is false will initiate the very helpful proof strategy known as *reduction to absurdity* or *indirect proof*. You may have used this strategy or seen it used without knowing its name because it is a common way of demonstrating a point. It relies on the insight that proving you are right sometimes can be accomplished by showing that you are not wrong. For example, see the "First version of the Ontological Argument" given in R-4.

The strategy of reduction to absurdity begins with *explicitly assuming you are wrong*. To this assumption you add whatever other premises are taken to be relevant and true in a given context. The objective of adding these other premises and drawing inferences from them is *to arrive at an absurd result*, such as a self-contradiction. When the absurd result is achieved, you then claim that the reason for the absurd result is the combination of premises along with the explicit assumption you first made. Then, because you feel more confident about the truth of the premises, you retain those as true, but you *reject your first assumption* as false. In effect, you have said, "Look, if I assume I'm wrong, this leads to a ridiculous result, so I'm not wrong."

Areas for Further Inquiry

• The strategy of indirect proof calls for the inference of a self-contradiction in order to guarantee that the initial assumption (or one of the premises) is false. Are there any kinds of absurdities, besides self-contradictions, that might serve? (See, for example, K-1.)

• Some ideas are so entrenched in our culture that when they operate as assumptions we often do not notice them. Just a few of the many challenged in various sections of this book include: Only humans have rights; the good of all is the sum of the good of each; capitalism and communism are radically different philosophically; time passes; a person's thoughts are inaccessible to others; every duty implies the obligation on the part of others not to interfere. Pick a section of the book and review it with nothing else in mind except locating and listing assumptions like those above. Then ask yourself whether they are true.

L-2   COMMON FALLACIES AND ERRORS OF REASONING

Question: How can I resist being deceived by someone's faulty reasoning?

Fact: Some deceptions are so common they have made names for themselves.

A Few Famous Fallacies

A *fallacy* is a mistaken argument, one that should not be accepted as a demonstration of the truth of its conclusion. Fallacies can result from a variety of causes. Some are simply mistakes, for example, errors in the application of sophisticated research methods. Some result from relying on false assumptions. Some occur because of formal (structural) errors in the way the argument's statements are put together. Here are some classic types of fallacies:

Appeal to ignorance.   Claiming that the mere absence of a reason for rejecting an opinion counts as a good reason to accept it.

Appeal to the mob.   Claiming that because "everyone" believes something it must be true.

Ad hominem attacks.   Claiming that supposed deficiencies in a person's character, heritage, sex, nationality, or some other aspect of personality are grounds for rejecting the truth of what the person says.

Equivocation.   Relying on the vagueness or ambiguity of words or phrases in order to demonstrate a point.

False cause.   Any of a group of fallacies based on false assumptions regarding causality (see N-8). For example, assuming that because event A happened after event B that B must be a cause of A.

97

Misuse of authority. Claiming that whatever an authoritative person says about anything (particularly anything outside his or her field of expertise) must be true.

Irrelevant appeal. Any of a group of fallacies, such as *misuse of authority,* which give as the reason for accepting a conclusion a rationale that is not demonstrably relevant to the truth or falsity of that conclusion. For example, appeal to celebrity status, appeal to what "everyone thinks," appeal to occult forces, appeal to astrological conditions, appeal to novelty or tradition.

The gambler's fallacy. Any of a group of fallacies that rely on errors regarding probability, such as that random events are causally connected.

Composition. Claiming that a characteristic of each part of a thing is necessarily a characteristic of the whole thing.

Division. Claiming that a characteristic of the whole thing is necessarily a characteristic of each of its parts.

Straw man fallacy. Claiming that by refuting the weakest of a series of arguments for a given claim, one has successfully refuted the claim.

Affirming the consequent. Fallaciously reasoning that if P, then Q. Q. Therefore, P. For example, the occurrence of A is sufficient to bring about an occurrence of B. B happened. So, A must have happened. Wrong; something else, C, might also be a sufficient condition for B, and this time it was C, not A, that caused B.

Denying the antecedent. Fallaciously reasoning that if P, then Q. Not P. Therefore, not Q. For example, the occurrence of X is sufficient to bring about an occurrence of Y. But X did not happen. So, Y will not happen." Wrong; something else, W, might also be a sufficient condition for Y, and W could lead to Y this time.

Playing with numbers. Any of a group of fallacies that misuses numbers, especially percentages and raw numbers, to exaggerate or diminish the apparent significance of the conclusion.

False dilemma. Claiming that there are no more options to consider, that a choice must be made between the options at hand, or that all of the options at hand are undesirable.

Begging the question. Relying on the truth of the intended conclusion as a basis to support one or more of an argument's premises. (This error is also sometimes called *reasoning in a circle.*)

Emotional appeal. Not strictly speaking an argument, this tactic plays on a person's emotions (fear, affection, anxiety, etc.) in order to get the person to do something, such as to buy an object or to agree with a given opinion or point of view.

Areas for Further Inquiry

• Joyously unending sources of diverse examples include advertising copy, letters to newspaper editors, and newspaper opinion columns.

• Learning about fallacies gives one the power to use them as well as the ability to avoid being deceived when others use them. This raises interesting questions about the ethics of using fallacies. The deliberate use of fallacies can certainly mislead people. Are people morally obligated to argue in reasonable and nonfallacious ways? What about scientists and teachers? Or what about government leaders and those who prepare newspapers and other sources we rely on for the truth? What about people who make their living in advertising, marketing, and sales?

L-3   JUSTIFIED, VALID, AND SOUND

Question: What makes an argument logical?
Guiding principle: Logical strength can depend either on the subject matter an argument talks about or on the ways in which the structural elements of an argument relate to each other.

Justified Inferences

To know whether the statement, "The Olympic Games have been held twice in Los Angeles," is true or false, you have to investigate the history of the Olympic Games. An argument designed to prove that this claim is true might go like this: "I just read an article on the history of the Olympic Games in an encyclopedia in my school library. Reading down the list of cities, I clearly remember that Los Angeles was mentioned only once when it hosted the Olympics in 1932. It is probably false, then, that the Olympics were held twice in Los Angeles."

Given just that much information, and no more, you might be willing to accept the conclusion that the games were only in Los Angeles once as true. After all, the evidence for it comes from a reliable source. On the other hand, you might ask when that encyclopedia was published. If the answer is before 1984, then you would surely question not its accuracy, but the completeness of its information. Also, having watched the 1984 Olympics on television, you might recall they were hosted in Los Angeles. By adding to the body of evidence available, you would be led to revise your opinion about your earlier conclusion. "Yes, the games were in Los Angeles twice." And, you would be justified in changing your view.

Building on this idea of being "justified" in holding a certain view, given one's level of background knowledge, let's say *an argument is justified or warranted if it is highly improbable that the conclusion would be false should all of the premises be true.* But *improbable* does not mean "impossible." As our example illustrates, conclusions of justified arguments are open to revision. (This was a point the skeptic often made in K-1 through K-3.)

Inductive Logic is the branch of logic that studies the *content* (conceptual and factual) relationships between the statements which make up different kinds of arguments with a view toward identifying objective methods and criteria for evaluating *justified arguments.*

Validity

Consider this line of reasoning: Every *D*-thing is an *E*-thing. Every *E*-thing has an associated *C*. Nothing that has an associated *C* can be an *F*-thing. So no *D*-thing is an *F*-thing. *Assuming that each of the three premises is true,* is there any way the conclusion could be false? The answer is: No. Given those premises, the conclusion *must* be true. Unlike the example about the Olympics, no new information (short of contradicting one of the premises) could possibly be discovered that would lead us to reject this conclusion, given the assumed truth of those premises. In a case like this, we will call the argument *valid.* Let us say *an argument is valid if it is impossible for all the premises to be true and the conclusion false.*

Notice that validity is independent of content. No matter how we fill in the expressions "*C*," "*D*-thing," "*E*-thing," and "*F*-thing," the argument remains valid. It is the same as: $3 + 3 = 6$. It doesn't matter if we are talking about daisies, dollars, or dentists. No matter what we substitute in, the argument remains valid. It is conceptually impossible, without changing the meanings of words, to find a counterexample for a valid argument. We cannot find a counterexample to "$3 + 3 = 6$" unless we change the meanings of one or more of those symbols (e.g., by thinking that "plus" means multiplication or that 6 stands for five discrete objects.)

> By the way, the example argument that led off this section exactly parallels the reasoning used in F-1 to set up the problem of free will and determinism. C is cause, D-things are human choices (decisions), E-things are events, and F-things are things that are free. It might be helpful to read F-1 as a series of examples about valid relationships.

Optional Advanced Note on Formal Logic.   Validity is said to depend on the relationships between the "formal elements" (that is, grammatical, syntactical, or structural elements) of an argument. Given what those elements are, there are different subbranches of formal logic that study them. In general, *deductive logic* studies the *formal* relationships between the statements that make up different kinds of arguments with a view toward identifying the criteria for an argument to be *valid.*

> Some of the subbranches of formal logic include: *propositional* logic, which addresses the logical relationships between simple assertive sentences, called *propositions* or *statements,* as these sentences are combined using words with the logical force of "and," "or," "not," and "if . . ., then"; *predicate logic,* which addresses the logical relationships between individual objects and classes of objects (or groups of objects designated by singular predicate expressions, such as E-thing); *the logic of relations* (sometimes called "the calculus of individuals" or "first order logic" or the "predicate calculus"), which expands the inquiry to include relationships between individual objects; *many-valued logic,* which explores the logic of multiple, rather than just two (true and false), "truth-values;" *modal logic,* which examines how expressions like, "It is possible that . . ." and, "It is necessary that . . ." affect validity; *deontic logic,* which examines logical relationships involving words such as *obligated, permitted, forbidden,* and *required;* second order logic, which examines the effect of applying the quantifiers "all" and "at least one" to the predicate and relational expressions themselves.

Soundness

In P-4 we proposed two tests to use in assessing arguments. Looking back at that section, you will recognize the first test (try to find a counterexample that makes the premises true but the conclusion false) is a way of getting at the "logical strength" of an argument—or, using our new concepts, seeing whether it is valid or justified. The second test was to inquire whether the premises were in fact all true. The word philosophers use to characterize arguments that pass both tests is *sound.* Let us say *an argument is sound if it meets two conditions: (1) it must be logical, meaning valid or justified, and (2) all its premises must in fact be true.*

An argument can fail to be sound in one of two ways, either by being illogical or by employing one or more false premises. Here is an example of an argument that is valid, but not sound: "John is my oldest child. Any successful thing my children accomplish makes me very proud. So, if John does something successful, it makes me very proud." *If* the two premises were true, then the conclusion would validly follow. Therefore, we would have to say the argument was "logically strong" to use the less precise vocabulary of P-4. But wait. Don't accept the argument as a proof of its conclusion. Why not? Because its first premise is false. I don't have a son named John. The argument is not *sound.*

The kinds of arguments we are looking to accept, if we are reasonable and rational people, are sound arguments sincerely offered; that is, offered in accord with the principles of rational argumentation (See P-4).

Areas for Further Inquiry

If you have never studied logic, you might wish to consider doing so. Besides being interesting, the skills in logic sharpen a person's native analytic abilities, making it much easier for the person to understand and evaluate the reasoning of others. Also, research into the logical structure of language, such as is occurring in computer science, is of major significance to many aspects of our technological society.

L-4   ANALOGIES AND MODELS

Question: What are the strengths and weaknesses of analogical reasoning?

Tools of the trade: Philosophers find analogies extremely useful although not very solid as proofs. Analogies help people understand the lesser known by relating them to the more familiar.

Comparisons and Analogical Reasoning

- Lacrosse is like hockey, except without the skates.
- Working for Smith is like picking cotton for Simon Legree.
- The best way to understand how to swing a baseball bat is to imagine swinging an ax at a tree trunk.
- Think of the world as a clock. Just as a clock could not have come into existence unless there was a watchmaker, so there must be a God who made this wonderfully complex world.

The last example is an *argument* by analogy. It proposes two parallel relationships: The world is to God as a clock is to a watchmaker. This relationship could be expressed: A is to B as C is to D. The earlier examples are comparisons on which arguments from analogy might be built. If we think of C and D as the more familiar phenomena, then what is being proposed in an argument from analogy is that we understand A's relationship to B on the basis of the *model* of C's relationship to D.

Each example above proposes that parallel relationships exist between something and its more familiar model. From this parallelism, a person might try to infer a number of things. (E.g., lacrosse, like hockey, involves putting some object into a goal. Smith treats his workers like slaves. When I swing a bat and make contact with the ball, I must have my arms extended.) But some of the conclusions might turn out to be false. (E.g., lacrosse players wear heavy protective pads all over. Smith does not pay his employees. I should hold onto the bat tightly, with both hands, after I hit the ball.)

Familiarity, Simplicity, Comprehensiveness, and Falsifiability

Assuming that in a given situation it is appropriate to use a model or an analogy to understand and reason about phenomena, important differences between alternative analogies help us evaluate them. What we are looking for is a relevant parallelism to use so we can infer things about less familiar phenomena on the basis of more familiar phenomena. This suggests the first criterion: *familiarity*. If you have only a vague idea of ice hockey or ax swinging, then you will have a harder time understanding lacrosse or baseball bat swinging. The more familiar the model, the more useful the analogy will be.

In terms of using the model to understand things, the *simpler* or less complicated the model is, the more readily it will be accepted as helpful. (For example, thinking of God as the great watchmaker is simpler—has fewer parts to it—than thinking of the maker of the world as a team of one hundred or more engineers and technicians who worked together on a major project. But what if we thought of the world as a spaceship?)

Being overly simple might be a liability, however, because a model must also be *comprehensive*. That is, the more phenomena an analogy helps us understand, the better it is. Consider how much more difficult it would be to understand a baseball swing if a separate comparison were used for (1) how the feet worked, (2) how the hips rotated, (3) how the hands moved, and so on. But the ax-swinging model is comprehensive because it accounts for all of these body movements; so it is superior to using three or more less comprehensive models.

Models often allow us to *predict* things. (E.g., if lacrosse is like hockey, then I should expect to find the field divided in half forming two equal areas, just as a hockey rink is divided with a red line in the middle.) If the prediction holds true, then the model is better than one that either does not allow us to make any predictions (e.g., if God is the divine watchmaker, then . . .) or a model that allows predictions that turn out false (e.g., if lacrosse is like soccer, then lacrosse players will not be allowed to use their hands). A model that allows predictions is *falsifiable*. That is, it is open to being refuted by an examination of the truth or falsity of the predictions it supports. A model that is open to being falsified is considered superior to one that is immune from falsifiability. For example, we

103

cannot falsify the analogy that says God is the divine watchmaker of the universe. Why? Because the analogy admits of no predictions and so nothing in human experience could be counted as *definitive evidence against* it. On this criterion, that is a weaker analogy than some other which allows for predictions and hence is subject to falsification on the basis of future experiences. The emphasis here is on how well the analogy allows for predictions, which in turn opens it up to *the possibility of being shown false.* If this possibility is entirely eliminated, then the analogy is considered of less value. Naturally, if an analogy admits of predictions that in fact turn out to be false, the analogy is not very good either. Good analogies are those that admit of predictions which turn out to be true. These analogies are falsi*fiable* but not falsified.

Strength of the Parallelism and Optimal Choice

In addition to evaluating analogical reasoning on the basis of the four considerations above, one can also examine the *strength* of the comparison. The more essential and pervasive the similarities are, the more credibility a conclusion based on those similarities will have. Two ways of critiquing the issue of the strength of the comparison are: (1) to suggest that the similarities noted are not important or essential but relatively superficial and irrelevant and (2) to suggest that in other important and essential ways crucial dissimilarities exist between the objects that the analogy compares. These concerns address the relevance and pervasiveness of the purported parallelism.

For example, how central or essential are the similarities between the world and a clock, or any machine? Are they strong enough to justify reasoning to the existence of a divine watchmaker? If so, what about the fact that human watchmakers die? Does that mean the divine craftsman might have died? Or recall that human watchmakers put their products on the shelf and leave them. Does that mean that the maker of the world might have moved on to other interests and left the world alone?

A second way to criticize a given analogy is by asking if it is the *optimal analogy* to use in a given situation. Is it *the best* analogy we have for understanding the phenomena in question? (E.g., what if we thought of lacrosse as soccer with sticks? What if working for Smith is more like being in the army? What if swinging a bat is more like a two-handed tennis backhand? What if the world is more like a living being, a plant, or an animal, than an inanimate machine?)

Areas for Further Inquiry

Analogical reasoning is *inductive.* The conclusion is made more or less probable by the truth of the premises; in this case, the adequacy of the suggested parallelism, as well as the simplicity, comprehensiveness, familiarity, and falsifiability of the model. Analogies are very useful for suggesting new directions of inquiry and for expanding the systematic quality and comprehensiveness of theories. But analogies are notoriously weak from the logical point of view—so weak that some thinkers try to avoid using them entirely. Question: Can anything ever be *proved* using an argument from analogy?

L-5   EMPIRICAL INVESTIGATIONS

Question: How can one draw inferences that go beyond the information in the premises?

Principle: Techniques of statistical analysis can support justified inductive inferences with high degrees of confidence.

Ampliative Inferences

Ampliative inferences draw conclusions that go beyond the evidence given in the premises. Such inferences are generally described as *inductive*. Some are justified, and others are not. A very simple kind of ampliative inference is *induction by enumeration* or *inductive generalization*. For example, every ball pulled out of the box so far has been white; so, the next ball to be pulled out of the box will be white. Obviously the conclusion does not necessarily follow from the premise, but the premise does lend plausibility—in the absence of any other information—to the conclusion. The lack of any apparent theoretical reason why the balls in that box should all be white, however, leads us to be wisely cautious about putting much confidence in the conclusion. One ball might happen to be another color.

The Hypothetico-Deductive Method

Significantly more complicated types of ampliative inferences form the basis for empirical research methods in the natural and behavioral sciences. The *hypothetico-deductive method*, for example, is used to provide explanations and predictions of natural phenomena. The hypothetico-deductive method can be outlined as follows: Begin with a general statement, called a *hypothesis*. (E.g., if a G is under conditions C_1, C_2, . . ., C_N, then it will behave in ways H.). Joined with the hypothesis are a number of statements describing particular states of affairs. (E.g., item a is a G, and it is now under conditions C_1, C_2, . . ., C_N.) From the hypothesis and the other statements, one *deduces* a prediction. (E.g., item a will behave in ways H.) Evidence is then gathered to determine the truth of this prediction. (E.g., the researcher examines a's behavior to see if it is behaving in ways H or not.) If the facts reveal that the prediction which was deduced is true, then the investigator is justified in

105

inductively concluding that the *hypothesis* is partially confirmed. If it turns out the prediction is *false*, the investigator is justified in *inductively* inferring that the *hypothesis* has been disconfirmed. In this case, the hypothesis is probably, but not necessarily, false. It might turn out that one of the other statements used along with the hypothesis to deduce the prediction is actually the false statement.

The logic of the inference from the general statement (the hypothesis) to the particular statement (the prediction) is independent of the temporal sequence of events. In other words, if we already know that *a* behaves in ways *H*, then—using the very same logical relationships—we can say that the hypothesis (the general statement) *explains* why the statement that *a* behaves in ways *H* is true. Because of this observation about the reasoning pattern used in the two situations, philosophers of science argue that the logic of "scientific explanation" and the logic of "scientific prediction" are essentially the same.

A Sketch of Empirical Research

Setting out to logically and systematically investigate an empirical question in a way that allows for intersubjective verifiability of both the results and the process inquiry involves a number of steps. (*Intersubjective verifiability* means the results can be verified by multiple investigators working independently of each other.)

1. Identify a problem of interest. For example, how does the study environment affect learning for college students?

2. Form a conjecture (or empirical hypothesis) regarding the problem. For example, college students who study in a distraction-limited environment retain more information than those who study in a distraction-intense environment.

3. Review the scientific literature in order to identify and examine relevant prior studies of similar or related hypotheses. For example, Jones, in 1988, discovered such and such about the effects of supervised study environments on high school students.

4. Identify the dependent, independent, control, moderator, and intervening variables in the study. For example, the *dependent variable* is student academic achievement; the *independent variable* is noise level in the study environment; the *control variables* are sex, age, class standing, GPA, program of study, and so on; the *moderator variable* is the number of minutes per day students report having studied; the *intervening variables* are the initial study skills of each student, outside events in students' lives that could affect attention, attitude toward college work, differential background knowledge of the subject being studied, and so on.

5. Set up operational definitions of each of the variables. For example, student achievement might be measured by test scores on validated, reliable, and standardized midterm and final course exams.

6. Assure that the proper controls will all be in place. At this point the researcher moves from the conceptual to the tangible. For example, volunteer students enrolled in a targeted college course are identified, and their consent to be subjects in this experiment is secured. Data about each student in the experiment regarding the control variables is gathered.

7. Design the data-gathering strategy. For example, subjects will be divided into six matched random groups; two groups will be put into each of three different study environments; study time will be controlled by . . ., and so on.

8. Construct measuring devices. For example, course examinations are written and pilot tested with other students not in the experiment, and each examination question is analyzed for validity.

9. Gather the data and monitor the experimental process. For example, the investigator has the examinations given and records test scores, takes readings from sound meters in each study environment, and so on.

10. Conduct a statistical analysis of the data and *inductively* draw inferences about what probably is the case regarding the hypothesis. For example, a correlational analysis or an analysis of variance is conducted, and it allows us to infer with a 95 percent level of confidence that it is not by chance that noise level in the study environment and a student's academic achievement are inversely related.

11. Write a research report and communicate the findings and the experimental methodology used to achieve them. For example, the study is published in a journal that is devoted to college level learning.

Statistical Analysis and Statistical Inference

A number of useful techniques of statistical analysis exist. Depending on how the experimental data is gathered and how the study is designed, some are more helpful than others in each given case. These methods of statistical analysis are designed to tell with what degree of confidence the *null hypothesis* can be ruled out. The null hypothesis is usually the assertion that the independent variable and the dependent variable are *not* at all related. In the above example, the null hypothesis was ruled out at the .05 confidence level. At times the confidence level can be .01 or even .001, depending on the kind of data collected, the research design used, and the method of statistical analysis applied.

Even at .001, the inference is still *inductive* and the conclusion still ampliative (goes beyond the premises). In the example above, the general conclusion goes well beyond the data gathered about the six groups of students. And what if the operational definitions were poor? What about the influence of the uncontrolled moderator variables? What about the selection of students in only

107

one particular course as a basis for making an inference regarding all college students? How well did the sample match the total student population?

Areas for Further Inquiry

The "riddle of induction" asks: How do we know that the future will be like the past, that similar causes have similar effects, or that induction is a reliable method of inference at all? If induction is used to justify our reliance on inductive methods, then aren't we reasoning in a circle?

NATURE

N-1   THE MIND-BODY PROBLEM

Question: What is real?

Insight: The uncritical commonsense view that reality is made up of a physical realm and a spiritual realm which are somehow independent yet connected is hopelessly vague, confused, and open to serious doubt.

The Commonsense Metaphysics of Ordinary Talk

First consideration.   Some characteristics people ascribe to things are physical or material, for example, location, length, height, weight, velocity, volume, viscosity, density, speed, chemical composition, and so on. These characteristics are generally regarded as (a) quantitative, (b) objective, and (c) open to observation and verification by others. This commonsense way of talking presumes a *physical* reality. A person's physical element—called the *body*—is generally regarded as being a material thing, subject to the same forces and physical and biochemical causality as any other organic part of the physical world.

Second consideration.   Some characteristics people ascribe to themselves and to each other are mental or spiritual, for example, people have emotions, thoughts, beliefs, hopes, ideas, conjectures, feelings, sensations, perceptions, attitudes. These characteristics are generally regarded as (a') qualitative, (b') subjective, and (c') knowable only through personal introspection.

This commonsense way of talking presumes a *mental* reality. A person's mental element—called the *mind*—is generally regarded as having no physical parts within itself and as being immune from the impact of external physical or biochemical causality.

Third consideration. Some commonsense descriptions imply that physical reality and mental reality can causally interact. For example, Kim dove into bed, implies three things:

1. Kim's body moved through space a certain distance at a certain velocity in a certain direction and was acted upon by the force of gravity so that it stopped on her bed.
2. Kim intended to make her body do 1.
3. 1 came about at least in part because of 2.

Take another example: His hormone imbalance is causing Joe to be depressed. This statement implies:

4. Hormone levels in Joe's body are outside normal ranges.
5. Mentally, Joe feels depressed.
6. 5 came about at least in part because of 4.

This commonsense way of talking presumes that mental reality can *cause changes to occur in* or *have a measurable impact on* physical reality, and physical reality can *cause changes to occur in* or *have an affect on* mental reality.

Some Problems with Common Sense

A critic of naive, unreflective belief in common sense could object: "First, the concept of *mind* is vague. Does it include the spiritual or religious idea of the soul or not? Although the mind is inside or near the brain, it is not clear if the commonsense view identifies the mind with that physical organ or conceptualizes the mind as something else that is nonphysical but can still interact with the brain.

"Second, the *interaction* of mind and body is not explained in either commonsense terms or scientific terms. How can the mental reality (which is thought to be entirely nonphysical) interact *causally* with the physical? If genuine causal interaction does exist, then the commonsense idea that the mind is entirely nonphysical will have to be revised. The location of the mind will also have to be identified, and its physical characteristics will have to be described.

"Third, causal explanations in the physical realm lead to *explanation, prediction, and control* (see L-5). By contrast, causal explanations in the mental realm lead, at best, to *understanding*. In commonsense terms we are given help in *appreciating* why normal people think what they think or feel what they feel, but we are not given a scientific *explanation* nor do the things said lead to scientific *prediction and control* of thoughts or feelings. If the mind and the body are subject to the same causal principles, then why have we no adequate science of the mental realm?

"Fourth, while a person is alive, the physical location of the mind seems at least vaguely identifiable—it is someplace in the person's body, probably in or around the brain. But given that the mind is immune from physical causality, does it seem logical, in commonsense terms, to infer that it will continue to exist after the body has died? And if so, where? For how long? And how does it perceive, or feel, without a body to input sensory data? However, if it is immune from the impact of physical causality, how then do we explain the third consideration above?"

Alternatives to Commonsense Confusion

Materialism (physicalism) holds that reality is entirely physical (see N-2). *Idealism (mentalism) holds that reality is entirely mental* (see N-3). *Dualism holds that reality is both physical and mental* (see N-4).

Metaphysics is the study of reality in general. It goes beyond the factual and theoretical inquiries of science. Metaphysics, in a sense, defines reality, and metaphysical discussions can change how we think about reality. Thus, metaphysics creates possibilities. What one thinks is possible depends on what one thinks might be real!

Areas for Further Inquiry

• Can the commonsense language of physical description and the commonsense language of mental description describe the same set of facts, or is that not possible? How do you suppose (before studying their positions) the answer to this question might affect the thinking of materialist, idealist, and dualist philosophers as they try to form a consistent and comprehensive theory regarding the nature of reality?

• What do you suppose (prior to studying the three positions) the likely implications of the three views named above will be for science, health care, ethics, education, government, religion, and finding meaning in life?

• In terms of knowledge about physical objects and other minds (see K-2 and K-3), what do you suppose (prior to studying their positions) the correlative theories of knowledge will be for materialist, idealist, and dualist philosophers?

Philosophical Role Playing

Defend—and where necessary improve—commonsense views from the four objections the critic made.

N-2 METAPHYSICAL MATERIALISM

Question: What is real?
Thesis: The hard fact is that reality is exclusively material!

A Basic Argument for Metaphysical Materialism

Commonsense talk presumes that reality has two sets of facts, physical and mental. The objective evidence of our senses tells us overwhelmingly that physical or material things, including our own bodies, are real. Reality is composed of only one set of facts. So, the only facts of reality are physical facts. Only physical descriptions can accurately and completely describe physical reality. Therefore, commonsense talk that presumes there is a mental realm of reality is unscientific, misleading, and inaccurate.

A Debate over What Is Real

A critic of the above position might object, "When we say things like 'Tim is frightened,' we are making an important factual statement. But we are not describing anything physical. So, reality does include mental facts."

The advocate might reply, "Truth is, saying 'Tim is frightened,' describes nothing at all. Now if you wish, we can talk about Tim's heart rate, the amount of adrenalin in his blood, his posture, his blood pressure, and so on, but other than these physical facts about Tim's body, there is no such thing as Tim's fear."

CRITIC: "I don't accept your analysis of feelings or emotions such as fear. But, frankly, motives (e.g., revenge) or character traits (e.g., courage) are even tougher cases. How do being envious, coy, proud, or noble fit into your theory?"

ADVOCATE: "In science there are complex dispositions, like being water soluble or being combustible. Motives or character traits are the same things, complex dispositions to behave in a certain way under certain conditions."

CRITIC: "I think there are still problems with this, but I want to voice a second concern I've been thinking about."

ADVOCATE: "Yes, what's that?"

CRITIC: "Careful, you almost admitted I was right before I even told you what I had in mind. And that is precisely the point. People do not always tell each other how they are feeling or what their opinions are. We keep some things to ourselves. How do unexpressed feelings and unstated ideas fit into the theory that reality is entirely physical?"

ADVOCATE: "Unspoken thoughts are myths. Can you name an unspoken thought? As soon as you name it, it has been spoken! The same goes for unexpressed feelings. Unless it is physical, it isn't real."

CRITIC: "When I'm hurting or experiencing pleasure, the irrefutable evidence of my own introspection assures me that the mental realm is real! I don't have to say what I am thinking or feeling for those things to be real. And when I finally do tell somebody I'm hurting, I am reporting something about myself, not creating something for the first time."

ADVOCATE: "First, any method that is subjective and cannot be verified is not a scientifically reliable method of saying anything. Second, no pain or pleasure exists in your mind. There is, however, your pain behavior or your pleasure behavior. I think it was Wittgenstein (1889–1951) who pointed out that humans have learned to say when they are hurt, instead of screaming as hurt animals do. But that only shows we have learned a more sophisticated kind of pain behavior."

> *Philosophical behaviorism* is the theory that statements presuming mental reality are entirely equivalent to statements describing physical reality. This theory of reality is closely related to the *phenomenalist* theory of knowledge. See K-2 and K-3.

A Different Approach to Materialism

The objective evidence of our senses tells us overwhelmingly that physical or material things, including our own bodies, are real. Reality is composed of only one set of facts. Commonsense talk presumes that reality has two sets of facts, physical and mental. So, the only facts of reality are physical facts. But, in contrast to the first argument, some mental descriptions do tell us important things. Therefore, such a mental description must be referring to the same set of facts as a set of physical descriptions.

> [*The identity theory* says that statements describing the mental realm actually refer to the *same set of facts* as sets of statements describing the physical characteristics of our brains.]

A Critic Looks at the Identity Theory

CRITIC: "I can't imagine how you could think that statements about mental reality *refer* to the same things as statements about physical facts. Think about it. First, statements about mental reality (e.g., I hate to lose) do not mean the same thing as sentences about physical reality (e.g., my brain is giving off gamma rays). Second, the evidence for each kind of sentence is different; specifically, introspection compared to the results of a brain-wave measurement test. And, third, I do not know that each is true in the same way. Particularly, I am certain of things like, I hate to lose, but I can only make probable inductive inferences about my brain waves."

ADVOCATE: "None of the three features you mentioned rule out the possibility that sentences about physical reality and sentences about mental reality actually *refer* or *denote* the same set of facts. Your observations only confirm what we already know about language, namely that facts can be described, demonstrated, and known in more than one way."

CRITIC: "There are other key differences too. Statements about mental reality imply only a vague location of mental events—that is, someplace in my head. Also sentences about my own mental reality are incorrigible, meaning not open to correction by the introduction of other evidence. And what's more, they are subjective, meaning they describe things only I can know."

ADVOCATE: "There are cases when a person is mistaken about his own so-called state of mind. Did anyone ever act abusively and insensitively toward you yet still sincerely say to you, 'I love you'?"

Areas of Further Inquiry

Philosophies of life that see immortality in terms of children or the improvement of the human condition seem compatible with physicalism. But physicalism, with its materialistic (in the sense of worldly) focus, suggests for many that life is meaningless—particularly in view of the vast history of human suffering and the ultimate death and bodily corruption that awaits us all. How do such reactions relate to the metaphysical positions being argued? What implications does metaphysical materialism really have for belief in the existence of souls, spirits, God, heaven, hell, and life after death?

Philosophical Role Playing

Suppose you were an educational psychologist who is a metaphysical materialist. What kinds of programs of education would you set up for teaching high school students world history? In particular, how would you define educational success in terms of "knowing" the subject? How might you treat so-called mental illness?

As the critic, which questions must the advocate still answer?

N-3   METAPHYSICAL IDEALISM

Question: What is real?
Thesis: Either dogmatic skepticism is true, or reality is entirely mental!

A Basic Argument for Metaphysical Idealism

We can know external objects exist in one of two ways, either by way of our senses or by way of reason. But our senses only tell us about our perceptions, not about the external world. (See K-2.) We have no knowledge of how a physical thing might act upon a spiritual entity. The evidence of introspection overwhelmingly and unmistakably reveals that our minds and ideas exist. Reality is composed of only one set of facts. Commonsense talk, though, presumes that reality has two sets of facts, physical and mental. So, the only facts of reality are mental facts. Only mental descriptions can accurately and completely describe mental reality. Therefore, commonsense talk that presumes a physical realm of reality is naive, unhelpful, inaccurate, and misguided.

A Debate over What Is Real

CRITIC: "Would you hold my textbook while I tie my shoes?"

ADVOCATE: "Sure."

CRITIC: "Thanks. You just refuted yourself. Your view implies that there are no physical objects! And don't disagree, or I'll knock you with the book you just held."

ADVOCATE: "Clever, but if you have any philosophical arguments that establish the existence of physical objects external to all minds, unthinking and independent of their being perceived, please let me hear them. I think it is silly to believe that numberless objects exist out there someplace serving no conceivable purpose and never being perceived by anyone, even God."

CRITIC: "I thought hitting you with the textbook was a solid idea! But now I'm not sure what to say. After all, once you grant dogmatic skepticism, then you cannot stop at denying that physical reality exists. You must also conclude that other minds are not real. Indeed, this argument ends in solipsism." (See K-3.) "So why are you even talking to me? I don't exist—at least not in your reality."

ADVOCATE: "Maybe solipsism is true! Then again, the defense for solipsism is at least clear. The defense for blind faith in the existence of a physical realm, given the force of the skeptic's arguments, is absurd. A person has to go where the logic leads."

A Different Approach to Idealism

We can know external objects exist in one of two ways, either by way of our senses or by way of reason. But our senses tell us only about our perceptions, not about the external world. (See K-2.) We have no knowledge of how a physical thing might act upon a spiritual thing. The evidence of in-

115

trospection overwhelmingly and unmistakably reveals that our minds and ideas exist. Reality is composed of only one set of facts. Commonsense talk, though, presumes that reality has two sets of facts, physical and mental. So, the only facts of reality are mental facts. But some physical descriptions are useful ways of talking. Therefore, such physical descriptions must be alternative ways of talking about the same set of mental facts as would be referred to by a corresponding set of mental descriptions.

Problems for Idealism

CRITIC: "Statements like 'This television set weighs thirty pounds' do not mean the same thing as statements such as, 'It appears to me that my arm muscles are straining to sustain their relative position beneath what appears to look like a television set suspended in what seems to be my hands.' In general, mental descriptions and physical descriptions do not mean the same thing. They are not known to be true using the same methods; nor does evidence for one kind necessarily count as evidence for the other. So how can you conclude that they refer to the same facts?"

ADVOCATE: "Statements can refer to the same facts even if the statements do not have the same meaning, even if they are known in different ways, and even if the evidence that supports one does not relate to the other. For each physical statement there is a corresponding mental statement that refers to the same fact about reality. We need not even change the way we talk so long as we understand that when we say *plants*, *animals*, *stars*, and so on are 'real,' we are referring to the fact that their reality consists in their being perceived by some mind. Reality contains nothing unperceived—if not by humans, then, at least, by God."

CRITIC: "But, what about the *problem of unperceived objects*? Suppose a flower drops a petal, but no one was ever in the meadow to see the flower bloom or the petal fall. Did the flower and its petal ever exist?"

ADVOCATE: "This is a serious problem. However, we can argue, much as contemporary subatomic physicists do, that the objects we conjecture to be real are in fact theoretical constructs that we suppose must exist because of the way things appear to our senses. If it is reasonable to claim the existence of constructs like the nuclear deterrent, social pressure, stress, manifest destiny, black holes, and equity, why can't the existence of computers, trucks, and autumn leaves be the same?"

CRITIC: "Flowers are not theoretical constructs. If they were, then what would the theoretical constructs of science be, supertheoretical constructs?"

ADVOCATE: "If you find problems with that response, a second and independent way to account for statements about unperceived objects would be to argue that God is constantly perceiving everything."

CRITIC: "I don't like appealing to a creator's existence as a strategy for proving that physical creation is real. If anything, that's backward. Also, whatever it might be like, God's 'perception' is radically different from human perception. For one, God has no sense organs. For another, God does not necessarily exist in our four-dimensional space-time manifold. And there are other problems. For example, if I saw the petal attached to the flower one day but fallen the next, doesn't my awareness constitute an entirely different kind of fact than God's continuous awareness of the flower and its petals?"

ADVOCATE: "Since you're still not convinced, may I suggest a third response. Why not treat unperceived objects in terms of counterfactual conditionals such as 'If someone had been in the proper place in the meadow at the proper time, that person would have seen the petal fall'?"

CRITIC: "There is a significant difference between *actual facts* (e.g., I saw it fall) and *possible facts* (e.g., I would have seen the petal fall, if such and such . . .). But I want to move ahead to the *problem of appearance and reality.* How do I tell the difference between those perceptions that I am only imagining and those that I can rely on to reveal something to me about the world?"

ADVOCATE: "One way to distinguish between appearance and reality is to argue that genuine sense perceptions are strong, orderly, coherent, and not subject to the control of my will. By contrast, imagination is faint, weak, unsteady, and can be altered at will."

Areas of Further Inquiry

•   Metaphysical idealists, like Berkeley (1685–1753), are often deeply committed to the principle that a philosophical theory must follow wherever logic leads. Idealism suggests it is irrational, in the sense of illogical, to believe in the existence of physical reality. If you disagree, can you point out the logical errors or false assumptions that cause all the problems for the idealist position?

•   Metaphysical idealism has often been regarded as consistent with certain religious views such as God's existence, the existence of spirits and souls, the possibility of a disembodied afterlife, the concept of reincarnation, and the idea that all spirits might someday merge into one. However, how does the physicality of something like Jesus' crucifixion or Job's body ulcers fit with such a spiritually oriented religious philosophy?

Philosophical Role Playing

As a physician who is a metaphysical idealist, how would you treat your various patients who come to you suffering from drug addiction,

117

malnutrition, AIDS, depression, job stress, or cancer? As an educator who is a metaphysical idealist, how would you design a program of reading instruction for second graders?

N-4   METAPHYSICAL DUALISM

Question: What is real?

Conjecture: Somehow reality must be partly mental and partly physical.

An Argument for Cartesian Dualism

The evidence of our senses tells us that the physical world is real. Introspection tells us that the mental world is real. So, both the physical and the mental are real. My experience of physical things is that they are unthinking objects that can be divided into parts. My experience of my mental self is that I am a thinking thing within which I can discern no parts or physical divisions. And so, the physical and mental realms of reality are separate and distinct. Only mental descriptions can describe the facts of the mental realm, and only physical descriptions can describe the facts of the physical realm. Therefore, the mental facts and physical facts form two mutually exclusive sets.

> This version of metaphysical dualism is one expression of the position called *Cartesian dualism*, named after Rene Descartes (1596–1650), the philosopher and mathematician who also gave us the Cartesian axis system.

A Debate Over What Is Real

CRITIC: "How can we be sure no more than two realms of reality exist? And how can we know the exact nature of each realm?"

ADVOCATE: "We should not multiply entities beyond necessity. We can say everything we need to say about reality by reference to these two realms. We know the physical realm through our senses, and we know the mental realm through the ideas in our minds."

CRITIC: "What am I? Am I a body or am I a mind?"

ADVOCATE: "Strictly speaking, you are your mind or spiritual self. Each of us is closely associated with, inside of, and closely connected to a body that we call our own. But our bodies can be diminished without our real self being hurt or compromised in any way. My immaterial self, which I can call my soul, can and will, therefore, continue to exist even if my body should die."

CRITIC: "I know when my body is cut, I feel pain. I know when I am happy, my body laughs. But if the two realms of reality are separate, distinct, and mutually exclusive, how do they interact?"

ADVOCATE: "Body and the soul do interact, meaning that the body can cause things to happen in the soul, and the soul can cause things to happen in the body. Maybe the two are connected somehow, or maybe physical changes cause the soul to have new ideas, or maybe changes occur in parallel at both the physical and spiritual level simultaneously. I don't really know how the two realms interact, but I'm sure they do."

CRITIC: "Hold it! You've only repeated the problem, not given me a solution. How do souls and bodies interact? How can something spiritual cause changes in things that are strictly material, and vice versa? If I were to accept this view, I would have to think of myself as an isolated ghost haunting a biological machine. If I am a wispy, solitary soul lurking mysteriously someplace inside a hulking body, I'm trapped in all the epistemological problems associated with dogmatic skepticism, including how knowledge of the external world and knowledge of other minds is possible. (See K-1 through K-3.)

"And another thing, calling everyone a soul does not resolve the problem of personal identity." (See N-5.) "How do you tell souls apart— say my soul from yours? How do we know souls don't merge? Where were our souls before our bodies were conceived? Where do they go after our bodies die? How do souls, which have no bodily organs, think, perceive, or communicate? If we are free-floating souls, there is no way of knowing who we are or what will become of us."

A Second Approach to Metaphysical Dualism

The evidence of our senses tells us that the physical world is real. Introspection tells us that the mental world is real. So, both the physical and the mental are real. Mental descriptions and physical descriptions may refer to the same facts. Somehow the mental and the physical realms interact. Therefore, the mental and the physical are both real but not necessarily separate, distinct, or mutually exclusive.

A Dual But Not Separate Reality

CRITIC: "Sounds to me as if we're back were we started in N-1. You've done an excellent job of expressing the problem. Now what is the solution? How do the two realms of reality interact?"

ADVOCATE: "Not true about no solution. The theoretical basis for explaining the interaction has not been fully worked out yet. But there are two promising avenues of inquiry. First, *personhood theory* advocates are working on defining human nature as a complex of physical and spiritual traits that are really two dimensions or aspects of a single unified being.

119

Persons have physical characteristics and mental characteristics. For example, they are a certain size, age, sex, and so on, and they can think, choose, perceive, feel, sense, reason, and so forth. The second approach is called *emergentism,* which is the theory that spiritual properties arise synergistically out of physical preconditions. For example, thought and self-consciousness arise out of the physical characteristics of the brain. In the same way, things like affection, team spirit, and so on emerge out of a definable combination of physical factors. We have only to complete the task of discovering these factors."

CRITIC: "The approaches you mentioned strongly suggest that the two realms are not separate but rather different sides of the same coin or further stages of the evolution of a single maturing reality. Does this imply that my spiritual self cannot exist without my physical self?"

Areas for Further Inquiry

• How is one's personal identity related to one's physical and spiritual aspects? Am I my body, my memories, my mind—all of these or none of them?

• What do phenomena such as telepathy, telekinesis, and precognition imply, if they are genuine, for the resolution of the mind-body problem?

• Religious beliefs about the afterlife seem compatible with the first basic approach given above, but how about with the second? If our spiritual self is only the other side of our physical self, then what happens when we die? Or maybe this entire way of thinking about religion is the problem. Perhaps salvation has nothing to do with a soul living after the death of the body. What *exactly* does the Scripture say? And how literal should we be in interpreting it, given serious philosophical objections?

Philosophical Role Playing

As a dualist physician, how would you treat a person who is an alcoholic? How would your approach differ if you were a philosophical materialist or a philosophical idealist? (Even if your treatment of the person did not change, your explanation of how the treatment is supposed to work would have changed.)

N-5   PERSONAL IDENTITY

Question: How is it that through all the changes in my life I remain myself?

Realization: My memories may fade, my consciousness may lapse, and my body may change in many ways, but through it all my personal identity is constant.

The Bodily Identity Criterion: "I Am My Body"

From birth till death a person has one and only one body. Socially we use physical evidence, such as pictures on a driver's license, to identify people and distinguish them from each other. So, for all practical purposes, I am my body.

A Case Against the Bodily Identity Criterion

First consideration. The question of personal identity is intended to be taken as a conceptual issue. Thus, making reference to social practice does not really address it. Moreover, if we actually took the bodily identity criterion seriously, then we would have to contend with a great deal of contrary evidence. For instance, an infant's body is radically different from an elderly person's body. Every cell from that original body has died and been replaced. Physical potentialities have emerged, been realized, and disappeared. Injuries and diseases have altered, or perhaps mutilated, parts of the body. Am I a different person if I have lost an arm in an accident? If so, why? Because of the physical loss or because of social and psychological factors relating to that physical change? The I-am-my-body view is too uncritical.

Second consideration. Consider the implications of the possibility of being cloned. If a person is cloned, would we then say that now there are two of that person? Or would we say there is the one person and a copy? And is the copy a person? If you answer, "Yes, to some degree," then how much? Does the clone have the same rights? Who takes priority in a conflict of interests, the person or the clone? Can the original person claim rights to use the clone's body for vital-organ transplants, but the clone not claim rights to save its life by using organs from the original? If the person should die, does the clone inherit ahead of other "blood" relatives? Do a person's possessions also belong to his clone? If a person and the person's clone could not be physically distinguished one from the other, which would be the real person? These questions regarding clones can only be answered by assuming some kind of personal identity distinct from bodily identity because my clone, in a real sense, is my body but not me.

Third consideration. Consider cases of severe psychic disorders such as multiple personalities. The only way to make sense of certain cases is to say there is only one body but more than one person. But, given the bodily identity criterion, we could not describe or explain these phenomena this way.

The Memory plus Psychic Continuity Criterion

Bodies change, but my memories are uniquely my own. My consciousness remains unaltered throughout my life. So, I am my personal consciousness with its accumulated memories.

121

A Case Against the Memory plus Psychic Continuity Criterion

First consideration. Memories are not reliable. People can fail to recall what they did or remember incorrectly. Memories can be destroyed by accidents, drugs, or surgery. We cannot identify a person with such a flimsy thing as a memory trace.

Second consideration. A person's consciousness can be interrupted or distorted by such events as coma, psychic delusions, hallucinations, and so on. Also a person's personality can change by becoming more mature, more developed, more or less capable of rational choice. Finally, some diseases and drugs alter or destroy a person's personality or consciousness: for example, steroids make a person angry and belligerent; Alzheimer's disease erodes a person's memories, consciousness, and former personality. In important ways people experiencing any of these phenomena cannot be said to be the same people they once were.

Combining the Bodily Identity Test with the Psychic Continuity Test

Let's not lose sight of our goals here. What we want is to be able to identify individual people and to distinguish one person from another. Whatever else is involved, each person can at least be described as a unique combination of psychic and physical phenomena, a body, and its set of conscious memories. Thus, a combination of both criteria, namely bodily identity and psychic continuity, are needed. Together they permit us to identify persons and distinguish one person from another. They help us with the problems of forgetfulness and the rights of clones.

A Case Against the Combined Criteria Approach

First consideration. If each test is fallible because of the reasons mentioned above, then how can they work together infallibly? What if my clone has my memories up to the point when he was generated? After that, our memories have gone our separate ways. Which of us is really me? What if the memories and personality of one of my ancestors were preserved in my genetic inheritance, and some drug or psychic disturbance caused them to emerge and take over my body? Who would I be then? If I had a brain transplant, assuming this includes all the stored memories and present consciousness of the donor, who would I be? Me because I still have my body, or the donor because I have the donor's memories and psychic continuity?

Areas for Further Inquiry

• Human beings are biological, social, and rational creatures who are influenced by a variety of factors such as their genetic inheritance, their environment, and their culture. How do assumptions regarding these influences impact the discussion of personal identity?

• What implications do each of the approaches to the problem of personal identity have for such issues as ethics, community responsibility, personal development, individual freedom, health care, education, and the government's role in guaranteeing basic rights?

• If an infant has no memories and a senile person has lost her memories, is the one not yet a person and the other no longer a person? In either case, what implications does this have for their human rights, such as their right to life?

• What implications does each approach to the problem of personal identity have for religious views regarding an afterlife? Give a consistent account of personal identity and the possibility of life after death. Does life after death imply a disembodied existence? Is a person a free-floating soul? At the end of time, will I receive a newly created, spiritual body as the Scripture says? If so, how will it be related to my former physical body? Will people be able to recognize me then, or I, them?

Philosophical Role Playing

Given either the bodily identity test or the memory test, but not both, write and defend a policy entitled "The Rights of Clones."

N-6   HUMAN NATURE

Question: Given what we are as human beings, should I spend my money on guns or butter?

Insight: As a human, I am a biological being, living in a certain physical, social, and cultural environment at a certain time and place in history. Unlike much of the rest of nature, I am capable of abstract thought, self-actualization, a wide range of emotions, and rational, autonomous choices. These facts influence how I think and act.

Normative Implications of Different Concepts of Human Nature

Philosophy of education, political philosophy, religion, and ethics await the answer to a simple question: What is human nature? As a thought experiment, let's try a couple of cases. First, suppose humans are essentially evil, selfish, insensitive, and aggressive. Societies would have to put constant external controls on everyone to keep our animal instincts to dominate one another in check. We might expect human society to be based on the assumption that the goal is to protect ourselves from each other and from our common enemies. In all probability, our education in such a society would be indoctrination; our laws would be severe; our religion would focus on exhorting us to tame our sinful selves; and our morality would include a heavy dose of legalistic attention to duty. To protect ourselves from *people just like us*, we had better spend our money on guns.

As an alternative, suppose humans beings are essentially good, rational, caring, sensitive beings capable of self-actualization, the appreciation of beauty, and thoughtful action motivated by a clear sense of mutual respect and civic responsibility. Human society might then be based on the goal of cooperative interaction to achieve shared goals, such as maximizing the opportunities for each person to achieve her or his highest potential. We might expect the goals of our education to be to nurture each individual's potentials for growth. Our laws would permit the maximum latitude for free expression. Our religion would be a celebration of love; and our morality—well maybe we wouldn't need to worry too much about morality since acting out of respect for others would be so natural. Given that *all humans were this way,* why not spend our money on butter; what need have we for guns?

Abbreviated Sketches of Representative Conceptions of Human Nature

Some thinkers offer pessimistic descriptions of human nature which suggest that if we allowed our instinctive aggressiveness and selfishness to go unchecked, we would find it very difficult to live in civilized harmony with one another. Hobbes (1588–1679), for example, describes the state of nature as if it were a war of each against all. In the Judeo-Christian tradition, humans have been characterized as being cursed and sinful creatures, fallen from grace, and in need of divine redemption to achieve salvation. Plato (428–348 B.C.) describes human beings as if they were at war within themselves, their rational selves trying to keep tight control over wild appetites and stampeding emotions. Seeing an actual war, such as the case of Viet Nam, often reinforces the view that human nature is essentially dark and malignant.

Other thinkers propose optimistic interpretations. Eastern traditions, such as Buddhism and Taoism, have strong strands of thought that emphasize the potential of human beings to overcome their initial selfishness and join with others in lives of harmony. Some strands of Christianity place greater emphasis on the Redemption than the Fall, on Easter than Good Friday. They speak to the potential of humans to live in the earthly kingdom of God, where charity and love prevail.

Even those who try to take a strictly descriptive look at human nature have difficulty denying that there are prescriptive or normative implications of their analyses. In examining the economic exploitation evident in capitalistic societies, Karl Marx (1818–1883), who saw himself as a scientific economist, described the human condition as one long history of class struggle resulting from the ownership of the means of production by only one subgroup in a society. Yet his response was not pessimism; it was optimism. Marx argued that eventually the means of production would be jointly owned by everyone in common, and at that time all class struggle would cease. For Marx the only rational thing to do was to work with, not against, this historical process.

With his interest in biology and natural history, Aristotle (384–322 B.C.) tended to emphasize the importance of the actualization of those distinctively human and positive potentials, such as the potential for rational thought. Like certain other species of animals, humans live in colonies that exhibit structure and organizations. As biological organisms, humans are subject to the laws of nature that define their instincts and control their behavior. However, among the distinctive potentialities of humans is our capability for rational thought, from which a person derives free choice and nobility of character. Since it is also in the natural order of things that an individual should tend to actualize its most distinctive characteristics, humans should naturally work to enhance their most distinctive feature, reason.

B. F. Skinner (b. 1904) advances the view that all behavior is explainable in terms of environment and conditioning. Although his approach, known more generally as *behaviorism,* need not deny genetic inheritance, it does claim that talk about *human nature and morality* is extremely misguided. We are what we are by virtue of where we have lived and how we have been conditioned. Behaviorism, as a form of hard determinism (see F-3), denies that free choices exist. Yet, even so, we can't avoid normative issues. The question of which behaviors, selfish or social, people *ought* to be conditioned to perform still arises.

Contrary to the determinist, others who seek an accurate descriptive basis for their theories conclude that human nature is entirely within our own control. *Existentialists,* such as Jean-Paul Sartre (1905–1980), argue that considering the tremendous unpredictability and array of options that are theoretically open to a person at any moment in time, the best way to understand human beings is as *absolutely free.* Through freedom we are able to define our own natures.

However, people flee from the crushing burden of freedom. To be constantly deciding what one wants to do and what one wants to be is an arduous responsibility. People try to hide behind their past decisions, calling them prior commitments and plans. But only the constant present is real, so one must constantly decide who one is and what one values. Some existentialists, seeing that no value exists except as individually defined, view life as an absurdity without exit. Others make a leap of faith into the exhilarating challenge of existence and seize the opportunity to create their own value and meaning.

And there are still other views of human nature operating in the world today as well. For example, *social Darwinism* emphasizes the principle of the survival of

125

the fittest, whether applied narrowly to one's own self-interest or ever more broadly to the interests of one's family, community, social group, or nation. *Secular humanism* is the view that the fair and reasonable thing to do, given a world as populated and troubled as our own, is to distribute all the human wealth and knowledge at one's disposal so as to help others survive and become self-sufficient and productive members of a local, national, or global community.

Areas for Further Inquiry

•   Is it possible to assess the descriptive accuracy of elements in various theories of human nature? For example, what counts as sufficient evidence to overturn such a theory? Is it possible to give an accurate and purely descriptive, non-normative analysis of the human condition?

•   What is your understanding of human nature? What are the scientific and metaphysical principles on which it is based? What are its ethical, governmental, educational, and religious implications?

•   Is war inevitable? Why? What does this say about human nature?

•   Will prejudice and racism ever end in our society? Why? What does this say about how we live and what we are?

Philosophical Role Playing

Imagine that you and a random 30 percent of the people where you live have just survived a nuclear disaster. All governmental services have been indefinitely interrupted. No communication with those who may not have been affected by the disaster is possible. Describe what would happen and what you would do in the period of time from right after the disaster through the next four months. Now, select any two of the theories of human nature sketched above and see how adopting each theory would alter your description.

N-7   TIME AND TIME TRAVEL

Question: What is time, and is time travel conceptually possible?
Insight: Time does not flow past us; we move in and through time.

The Dynamic View of Time

ADVOCATE OF THE *DYNAMIC* VIEW OF TIME: "Like a wind rushing by our faces, time whisks from the past to the future, pausing for only the smallest instant in this moment we call the present. The past is unreal, and the events it contains are no more. The future is unreal, and the events that will become are not yet. Only the fleeting present—that place where past and future join—is real. And even that reality is lost into the past as quickly as it is conceived. Think, you who flit on life's stage for your one tiny moment of existence, how should you use what precious little time you have?"

CRITIC: "Your analogies are charming, but your thinking is confused. If only the present is real, how can we measure the *passage of time?* Any measurement must be against some external standard. But do you want to argue that some kind of time outside of time exists? Also consider the present. According to you, it is the point at which the unreal past touches the unreal future. In that case it is so infinitesimally tiny as to have no duration in itself. Thus, the present is unreal too. But if time is the accumulation of present moments, you might as well say that time is entirely unreal. There is no *past, future,* or *present.*"

The Static View of Time

ADVOCATE OF THE *STATIC* VIEW OF TIME: "Time doesn't pass. We do. We move through time as if we were driving along an interstate highway. The highway stretches ahead of us and behind us to places we may never visit. We get on the highway at birth and exit at death. We move along, like those in the cars beside us, at a constant rate of speed. So, looking from car to car it seems we are not moving, but looking at the mileposts flashing by, like the days of our lives, we are moving steadily. Along this highway are places that came *before* or *after* or *simultaneously* with others. The past and future are real and relative, not unreal and absolute."

CRITIC: "You make it sound as if all I have to do is make a U-turn and I can go back in time. That's absurd. Also, by your analogy, if I step on the accelerator, I can shoot ahead of the other cars and, in effect, speed myself into the future. That is also absurd.

"Your problem is that you are thinking of time as analogous to your concept of space. However, our movement in space from one place to another does not imply that we can move in time from one present to another."

ADVOCATE: "We do move in time, all together at the same rate, from one present to another. If that were not so, then no changes in our perception, or in reality itself, would ever be possible."

Two Time-Travel Conjectures

ADVOCATE: "I am right to think of time exactly the way I think of space. Science says time is one aspect of a unified four-dimensional space-time reality. *Think of space-time as an unbounded emptiness spreading in four dimensions from a center that is the here and now.* People and things exist at various coordinates in space-time. Things in future or past time are equally as real as things in present time but in other places. So I don't think time travel is absurd. In fact I know of two time travel conjectures, a weaker one and a stronger one."

The weak time travel conjecture. Since we are now moving through time at a uniform velocity, as measured by our chronometers (clocks), it is conceptually possible to *speed up or slow down that forward velocity* hence locating ourselves in some other part *of the future* than where we would be found had we maintained our current pace.

The strong time travel conjecture. If it is possible to move back and forth from one space to another space, and if time is simply a fourth such dimension, then it is possible in principle to move *back and forth* in the time dimension as well as in any of the three space dimensions.

Implications of the Time-Travel Conjectures

The suggestion of the weak conjecture is that a time traveler might enter a time travel device at time T, as measured by a clock external to the time travel device set at *external time T*. Then the time traveler would emerge from the time device at some later external time $T + X$, where X is how long, measured in external time, the traveler stayed in the time machine. Thus, $T + X$ is later than T. The only two changes possible would be that the time traveler's *personal time (PT)* changed at a velocity that was either faster or slower than the pace of *external time (ET)*. Thus, $PT + X$ is not equal to $ET + X$. In the weak conjecture, the implications are that the change was in *the same temporal direction as ET* and that *some amount PT, not equal to X, was consumed* during the change.

By contrast, the strong conjecture suggests that a time traveler could move into ET earlier than T. Here, too, some amount of PT is consumed.

Think of the present consciousness of the time traveler. If we use a line to represent, or trace, the PT of the time traveler, the line will be *unbroken* under both conjectures. The time traveler will *age* at the normal rate; however in the first, the aging may appear faster or slower than it would appear in ET. In the second conjecture, the aging process, which by definition happens at a normal pace as measured in PT, may be completed at some time ET earlier than T.

Facione's Seven Untimely Metaphysical Laws of Time Travel

Not wanting to embarrass any philosopher with the burden of even the most casual association with such bizarre, if not absurd and indefensible, opinions, I offer the following seven so-called laws under my own name.

1. *Past events in ET or PT cannot be altered.* This assumption is necessary to avoid the self-contradictions and causal absurdities that arise in stories where people go back and do something to alter or rewrite historical events (such as preventing some historical figure from coming to power or rendering their own existence impossible).

2. *The time traveler's PT, or existential line, must remain unbroken.* This is to assure that each time traveler continues to exist and maintains his or her unique personal identity throughout all *ET* jumps.

3. *The laws of physics, chemistry, biology and, in general, the causal laws of nature cannot be violated.* This guarantees that what the time traveler does is consistent with other scientific understandings. A time traveler cannot, for example, serve as one of her own ancestors.

4. *Where a time traveler enters the time-travel device is where he exits it.* Unless the time-travel device is also equipped to move from place to place, we must presume that the only dimension that it travels through is the temporal one.

5. *The time-travel device and everything in it is located in the same ET as the time traveler.* Unless the time-travel device is equipped to be sent off without an occupant, once a time move is made, the time-travel device stays with the traveler, like a car with its driver.

6. *Each appearance of the time traveler in ET is real at any moment T.* Under the second conjecture, a time traveler can "loop back" and be present at time T at more than one place. However T, a slice of space-time, happens only once in *ET*. So, the time traveler must be present at each of her places when T occurs. For example, if I travel five minutes back in time to watch myself write this, then while I am writing this I am also visible standing next to myself watching myself. *Looping* my *PT* back through an *ET* moment more than once cannot arise under the first conjecture.

7. *Everything must be brought into existence by something other than itself.* This rules out *closed loops*. Looping *PT* back through a given moment of *ET* suggests the possibility of *closed loops*. For example, a person goes back in time and provides himself with information about the future which leads him to invent a time-travel device. Or he serves as all of his own ancestors. Or he gives someone a gift from the future that he had received from that same person in the past. But *closed* loops, although explainable in each of their steps, are not explainable in their entirety without violating the principle that nothing comes from nothing. The knowledge must originate from some place. The unique genetic material must come from someplace. The gift must come from someplace. *Open* loops are not ruled out. For example, I can go back and advise myself about investing in the stock market.

Areas for Further Inquiry

• There are many time-travel stories, but are they logically consistent?

• Can God know propositions about the future? (See R-3.)

• Can a time traveler go back in time and change an abstract idea? Or are abstract ideas unchanging and "timeless?"

• What does theoretical physics say about the conceptual possibility of the weak and strong time-travel conjectures?

N-8   THE CONCEPT OF CAUSALITY

Question: Why?

Strategic realization: If we could know when two events, A and B, are related such that B is the result of cause A, then we could explain and predict B by reference to the occurrence of A. And if we could control the occurrences of A, then we could control the occurrences of B.

Understanding and Explaining

Certain lawlike generalizations can be used in conjunction with descriptions of current or possible states of affairs in order to infer that some other state of affairs will result. This logical relationship is called an *explanation* or *a scientific prediction* of the resulting state of affairs. (See L-5.) The conjunction of the lawlike generalization and the initial conditions can be considered a *cause* of the *resulting* state of affairs. Identifying a cause is one way to answer the question "Why?" For example, why did the stone fall to the earth when I released it from my grip? Because nothing prevented gravity from accelerating the stone toward the earth. Why did the plant wither? Because its root system was so damaged that an insufficient number of water molecules were absorbed, and it dehydrated.

Another way to understand and respond to the question, Why? is to ascribe motives or intentions to persons. For example, Jill was motivated by her love for her child. John failed because he wanted to show his parents that he didn't care. I decided to sell the car for three reasons; it was old, small, and ugly. I had hoped to save a few dollars. *Motives, intentions, goals, purposes* and, in general, the kinds of things people call *reasons why they did things* are *not* generally considered *causes*. They are, in a broad sense, *responsible factors* that help us *understand* or *appreciate* why a person does something. However, reference to these kinds of factors do not permit us to *explain and predict* a normal person's behavior. For example, knowing that John intends to demonstrate his indifference to his parents by failing does not permit one to predict exactly what form that demonstration will take. It is generally believed that adult humans making rational decisions behave in ways that can be understood, but not always predicted. (See F-4 and F-5.)

Microexplanation and Macroexplanation

The kinds of explanations associated with the scientific program of discovering and describing causal interactions are *microexplanations*. As an illustration, the chemical imbalance in the water made the litmus paper turn that color. If each fact can be explained in such terms, then we consider the scientific enterprise successful. However, at times people seek *macroexplanations*. They ask questions that go beyond inquiring into why any given fact occurs. For example, they ask things like: Why is there something rather than nothing, or how do we explain the existence of the universe or of reality in total? (E.g., see R-6.) At times, people also add a purposive dimension to their question. For example, they ask what is the reason, plan, or purpose of creation? (E.g., see E-6.) In seeking macroexplanations, people are going beyond science to the level philosophers call metaphysics.

Some philosophers argue that the questions which solicit macroexplanations, along with any answers that might be proposed to those questions, are, by definition, nonsense—that is, they go beyond what can possibly be answered using the methods of empirical, inductive investigation (sketched in L-5). Others regard such questions as meaningful but purely speculative in the negative sense that no way exists to objectively judge which possible answer is correct. Still others regard them as meaningful questions that can be responded to by the articulation of a comprehensive world view. (See T-3.) But none of these ways of responding to the quest for macroexplanations sees the answer in terms of causality in the strictly scientific sense.

Necessary and Sufficient Conditions

A cause can be helpfully thought of as either a necessary or a sufficient condition for something to occur. An occurrence of A is said to be a *sufficient condition* for the occurrence of B if it is not possible that A should occur and B not occur. For example, withdrawal of oxygen from the adult human brain at normal body temperatures for a period greater than ten minutes is sufficient for the occurrence of brain death.

An occurrence of X is said to be a *necessary condition* for the occurrence of Y if it is not possible that Y should have occurred and X not have occurred. For example, an increase in heat, along with no increase in the volume of a closed container, are two necessary conditions for an increase in the pressure of a gas within that container.

Temporal Sequence and Correlation

Temporal sequence, once thought to be an essential element in causality, turns out not to be a helpful consideration. Notice the example of gravity mentioned above. The *presence* of the causal agent, in contrast to its absence, also turns out not to be a helpful consideration. Notice the examples about the withdrawal of oxygen and water. *Correlation* by itself is also troublesome. For example, each morning before I drive to work I eat a hearty breakfast. But eating breakfast does not *cause* me to drive to work.

Correlation may be difficult to distinguish from causal *connection* in practice. For example, one might observe a correlation between regular jogging and better than average cardiovascular ability without being able to declare that the two are causally connected. Some thinkers argue that the difference lies in the fact that we are *less sure* of correlations than causes. But the inferences used to discover these relationships support both with equal levels of confidence. (See L-5.) A more promising approach to distinguishing the two is on the basis of the existence of a *covering theory*. (See T-2.) In the case of breakfast and driving to work, I know of no theoretical reason, no lawlike generalization, that plausibly connects the two facts so that the eating becomes either a necessary or sufficient condition for driving to work. But, given what we now know about exercise physiology, it is plausible to suppose that regular jogging *causes* and sustains an improvement in one's cardiovascular ability.

Areas for Further Inquiry

• What about social or historical causes? Does it make sense, in terms of the understanding of causality, scientific explanation, and scientific prediction to ask: What were the causes of the Civil War? Or to explore, What were the causes of this company's economic success last quarter?

• A *counterfactual conditional* asserts that had some key factor been other than it was, different results would have occurred than did occur. What is the relationship between knowing the causes of a fact and being able to decide if a counterfactual conditional about the fact is true?

• If observation alters reality, as in subatomic physics or in politics, can we ever describe and predict specific results with certainty?

132

RELIGION

R-1   THE CONCEPT OF GOD

Question: What is God?

Proposition: God is complete metaphysical and moral perfection.

The "God" Concept

God's existence or nonexistence is not trivial, unimportant, or inconsequential. It is widely believed that God's existence has profound implications for religion, morality, the meaningfulness of human existence, indeed, virtually every aspect of our lives here and after death as well. Thus, when the question of God's existence arises, emotions often cloud the conversation. This makes philosophical clarity and precision regarding what is being discussed even more crucial.

Try as you might, you cannot avoid the issue. For *practical* purposes, there are only two views: *theism* (I believe God exists) or *atheism* (I believe God does not exist). *Agnosticism* (I'm not sure whether God exists) comes to the same thing in terms of practical day-to-day living, as either theism or atheism, in most cases atheism.

However, when a person professes faith in God, what exactly is the person saying he or she believes in? The concept of God has been known to vary greatly within and between different historical eras, cultures, and religions. God has been thought of as an animal, a human, or a spirit. In some branches of Hinduism and in the tribal religions of South America and Africa, people believe in the existence of multiple deities. Other religions interpret the very same phenomena that give rise to these beliefs differently, saying they are multiple manifestations of one God. The Greeks and Romans developed elaborate mythologies to describe and explain the interactions of the many goddesses and gods they thought populated the universe. Seeing the pain in our lives, some argue there are two divine forces at war in the universe: one a force for good; the other a force for evil. Others offer very abstract concepts of God; for example, Plato (428–328 B.C.) regarded God as reason. In the Hebrew Scriptures, God declines to clarify matters for us, saying instead that people should refer to him as "I am." In John's Gospel, God is the Word. Aquinas (1224–1274) identified God as pure existence. Others offer very tangible images. Jesus called God "Father." At one point in the Bible, God is described as experiencing typical human emotions and reactions, such as being vengeful or jealous, at another place He is gracious, loving, and forgiving. God has often been thought of as a single gender. In the past 2,000 to 4,000 years it has been "He," but in prehistoric times it was often "She."

For Inquiry. A major problem in the philosophy of religion is to clarify the exact meaning of the question, "Does God exist?"

Attributes of the Divine

Within the Judeo-Christian tradition(s), a large number of different characteristics have been attributed to God. The following list may not be complete, but its lack of completeness is not the most difficult thing about it. The real problem is that the list appears to contain self-contradictory descriptions. But how can God exist if He cannot be consistently described?

For Inquiry. How can God be all of the following?

Transcendent: Beyond all reality and existing outside of space and time.

Imminent: Intimately present in reality at all times and in all places.

One: A unity, an individual entity with a singular identity.

Unique: The only God, one of a kind.

Living: Having life, not being an inanimate thing.

Many-personed: Having more than one person within the Divine Unity (e.g., Father, Son, and Holy Spirit).

Everlasting: Without start or ending, not created and immune from death.

Nonphysical: Without a body or physical substance of any kind.

Gendered: Male.

Omnipotent: All-powerful, able to do anything that can be consistently described (but not something that is a self-contradiction in terms).

Omniscient: All-knowing, aware of everything that was and is happening. (Some believe that God knows the future as well.)

Benevolent: All-good, always acting out of concern for the interests of creation.

Moral: Completely ethical—always acting in accord with principles humans would recognize as moral (e.g., God is just).

Loving:	Concerned and caring in regard to creation collectively and individually; specifically, able to love humans.
Lovable:	Capable of being loved by human beings.
Purposive:	Acting with goals in mind; not a wild, uncontrolled force loose in the universe. (Things happen according to His plan or at least because He has allowed them to be the way they are.)
Wise:	Possessing the highest wisdom, fully aware and appreciative of the finitude of created things.
Perfect:	The best possible combination of all of the above characteristics and other virtues as well; having complete integrity with no existential flaws or character blemishes of any kind whatsoever.
Sacred:	Holy and totally awe inspiring.
Knowable:	Capable of being at least partially known by human beings either through direct revelation, mystical contact, the medium of others (prophets or angels), or the messages given to humans through inspired texts.
Ineffable:	Beyond being described in words. (God is the gracious mystery giving reality and meaning to everything else.)

Faith, Reason, and the Oneness of Truth

A majority of people living today claim to believe in God's existence. But when it comes to talking about what that means, many fall back to the unreflective answers they memorized in their youth, or else, in frustration, they declare themselves unable or unwilling to discuss seriously the conceptual problems associated with their religious faith. They try, as it were, to put a wall between the realm of faith and the realm of reason. But the wall does not hold up. Truth, whether under the correspondence theory or the coherence theory (see K-4), is one: The beliefs we hold in one area should be consistent with those we hold in another, or that at least is the presumption we must begin from if we are to make any progress in knowledge and wisdom. That is what it means to say "truth is one."

Some who believe that truth is one say this implies an *essential and necessary war between reason and faith.* It is not for humans to be able to demonstrate with their feeble minds what God is or that God exists. Since truth is one, we should reject what our scientists tell us if their claims contradict the sacred books that contain the revealed word of God.

Taking it a step further, some hold that ignorance is desirable. If humans could actually prove that God existed, then faith would not be necessary. But, without faith, there could be no salvation! God wants us, they say, not to be certain. God wants us to make a trusting leap of faith, to abandon reason and rely on the Almighty's merciful love. Religion means belief in the absence of sufficient evidence. It is sinful folly to try to turn religion into science.

Others who maintain that truth is one believe that the truths of faith and *the*

135

truths of reason, including science, can ultimately be reconciled in a unified consistent theory of reality. Such a theory would be a complete world view. It would tie together metaphysics, epistemology, ethics, religion, and science. It would tell us not only what life is, but how best to live it. Advocates of this approach ask: If God's greatest gift to human beings is rationality, why would God set it up so that we can come to Him only by being irrational?

Then, too, some think that truth is not one. Conveniently, this lets them believe inconsistent things, and it also relieves them of the intellectual responsibility of having to make sense of anything. Philosophers regard this as intellectually dishonest and unethical.

Arcas for Further Inquiry

• Is all truth one? Does being religious mean that one must find a unified world view or deny the power of reason and the validity of science?

• Religious close-mindedness, anti-intellectualism, and self-righteous intolerance have deep roots in American culture, going back to the first European settlers. Then, too, the smug sophistication of those who sneer at religious faith can be equally infuriating. In what sense does the truth set us free? Do you accept the principle that, for all practical purposes, there are only two views: atheism or theism? Is Buddhism a counterexample?

• Some argue that without God nothing would have objective value, and human existence would ultimately be a meaningless absurdity. What is the relationship between religious faith and ethics?

Philosophical Role Playing

Assuming the attributes listed above, modify each as necessary in order to arrive at a consistent description of the Judeo-Christian God.

R-2   THE DESIGN ARGUMENT

Question: Does God exist?

Reflection: The order and organization evident in the natural universe is awe inspiring and leads one naturally to wonder at the majesty and power of the mind that designed and created such intricate beauty.

A Version of the Design Argument

Science has shown considerable evidence of intricate order, interconnectedness, and complex organization in nature. The best way to understand and explain that order is by analogy to the order that human intelligence imposes when a person designs and builds something. Thus, it is probable that there is an intelligent planner of the natural universe.

The Case Against the Design Argument

First consideration.   There are problems with the quality of the evidence in support of the first premise. This evidence is inconclusive at best. During the long process of evolution, some life forms have not adapted well and became extinct; certain bodily organs—like the appendix—seem to have no function.

Second consideration.   The analogy between things in nature and things made by people fails in several ways. One important difference is regarding the purposefulness of the things in nature. When a human makes something, it is considered to have a purpose *of or for its maker.* But what purpose *of or for their maker* do the things in the natural universe serve?

Third consideration.   The best explanation of the apparent order in the universe might be by analogy to a divine planner, but it might be better to think of the universe as if it were generated (given birth perhaps by some alien forms of life) rather than built (made or constructed). It might be better to think of life on earth as evidence suggesting the earth was once visited by space travelers rather than as evidence for an intelligent planner. It might be better to explain *each individual thing* in terms of the empirical sciences (chemistry, biology, genetics, geology, and physics) rather than trying to explain *the whole of nature* in terms of an intelligent planner. In the final analysis, though, this argument is only an analogy, and analogies are often not conclusive. (See L-4.)

Fourth consideration.   Even if an intelligent planner designed the universe, this does not imply that this designer was the same personal and transcendent God worshiped in the Judeo-Christian religions. It does not prove that the designer is loving, omniscient, omnipotent, or omnipresent. It does not prove that the designer still exists or still cares about the universe.

Areas for Further Inquiry

• The design argument seems to rely on the metaphysical assumption that nature is goal directed. Is this assumption true?

• When the design argument is used, what purposes might it be intended to serve? Is it really an effort to persuade nonbelievers that God exists?

• Is "God exists" only an expression of an *attitude* toward nature, not of an empirical hypothesis? Does a crucial experiment exist such that a sophisticated religious person would agree ahead of time to accept the results as indicating, once and for all, whether God exists?

• Does the theory of evolution falsify the design argument?

R-3   THE PROBLEM OF FREEDOM

Question: Does God exist?

Conceptual conflict: Human freedom, understood as the ability to create one's own future through a series of choices, is incompatible with the existence of a God, conceived of as an all-knowing divinity.

A Case That Divine Foreknowledge Is Inconsistent with Human Freedom

God is all-knowing. As all-knowing, God knows the truth or falsehood of all statements. Statements can be about the future as well as the past or present. So, God knows the future even before it happens. This implies that God knows what I will choose even before I choose it. Therefore, I am not free; I must choose what God knows I will choose. Given the fact that I am free, there can be no all-knowing God.

A Debate over the Argument

CRITIC: "Foreknowledge does not imply exercising control. I can know what will happen and why but that does not mean I made it happen."

ADVOCATE: "God designed the universe." (See R-2.) "He or She may not be continually influencing each and every choice; all the conditions were prearranged. Everything happens the way it does because God arranged it."

CRITIC: "That means everything is predetermined, and so free choice is random, unpredictable behavior, or it is totally illusory." (See F-2).

ADVOCATE: "Our experience of rational, free choice is not one of randomness; rather it is of deliberation, consideration, evaluation of options, and decision making. The redefinition does not fit our experience. And besides, if God is all-good, God would not deceive us with regard to freedom."

CRITIC: "Your final conclusion does not follow. Being all-knowing does not imply knowing the future. One can know only what is and what was, not what will be."

ADVOCATE: "This presumes a theory of time in which the future is not yet real. But if space-time is a static four-dimensional manifold, then the time reference of a given statement relates to its location in that manifold. In principle, if knowledge can be had of any time-referenced statement, it can be had of every time-referenced statement." (See N-7.)

A Case That Divine Omnipotence Is Inconsistent with Human Freedom

God is all-powerful. God controls human actions. So, human actions are predetermined, not free. But human actions are free—that's given. So, there is no all-powerful God.

A Debate over the Argument

CRITIC: "Why do you think God controls human actions?"

ADVOCATE: "If I might, let me use Scripture as a weapon against the theist. The Scriptures give us several examples: God can harden men's hearts; God causes some people (like Judas) to serve divine purposes; only those who are given the gift of grace can be saved; some are predestined to everlasting happiness, and others are not preselected for this reward."

CRITIC: "First I think your interpretations of the Scriptures are incorrect. God did not take free choice away when She or He did any of these things. Second, to be *capable* of controlling all things is not the same as *actually* controlling them. God could, but does not, destroy human freedom by predetermining human choices. And third, in the final analysis, rather than deny that God exists, I am prepared to say freedom is an illusion!"

A Case That Human Dignity Is Inconsistent with God as Creator

Suppose God, the all-knowing and all-powerful maker of the universe, existed. By analogy, humans would have no more real freedom than a machine has. A computer can only do what its maker programmed it to do. But human dignity demands that humans be genuinely free and capable of self-determination. So, to affirm human dignity, we must deny God's existence.

Possible Objections to the Argument

CRITIC: "First, God could have created humans with free will and human dignity, if He or She wanted to. That's what being all-powerful implies. Second, your analogy is weak because humans are not machines. Unlike machines, humans are capable of thought, creativity, humor, and emotion. Third, your analogy is weak because if God can create things that can make free, informed, rational decisions—namely humans— perhaps someday humans will be able to make machines that are capable of thinking and rational decision making." (See K-5.)

Areas for Further Inquiry

• Are human dignity and God's existence mutually exclusive? What instructive parallels can be drawn between the God-and-human-freedom issue and the relationship between humans and the intelligent computers they might someday build?

• Are there any other attributes of God, besides being omniscient, omnipotent, and creative, which conflict with our understanding of human nature?

Philosophical Role Playing

As the critic, press the objections to the first argument further. Then take the side of the advocate and defend the second and third arguments from the unanswered objections the critic raises.

R-4 THE ONTOLOGICAL ARGUMENT

Question: Does God exist?

Proposition: God is supreme perfection and, therefore, must be real.

A First Version of the Ontological Argument

Assume that a being than which nothing more perfect can be thought existed only in the mind and not in reality. We can think of such a being as existing in reality. Existing in reality is more perfect than existing in the mind only. So we can think of something more perfect than that being than which nothing more perfect can be conceived. Since this result is a self-contradiction, it follows that the initial assumption must be false. Therefore, the being than which nothing more perfect can be thought exists in reality, not just in the mind.

> The Ontological argument is historically associated with the eleventh century abbot St. Anselm (1033–1109). The proof strategy used above is called "indirect proof," and it is explained in L-1.

A Debate Regarding the Argument

"Why not a perfect island?" declared Anselm's contemporary, Gaunilo. "Or why not a perfect computer, a perfect jump shot, or a perfect anything? Does describing something as 'perfect' imply that it, therefore, exists?"

"No," said Anselm, with a kindly, paternal smile, "the argument only applies to God!"

"Why?" inquired Gaunilo, scowling beneath his monk's hood.

"Because God is a being the nonexistence of which cannot be consistently thought. However, we can imagine the nonexistence of a perfect island, a perfect jump shot, or a perfect anything else . . ."

A Second Version of the Ontological Argument

God, by definition, possesses not just some, but *all* perfections. When we try to imagine God as not existing, we find the concept self-contradictory. So, existence is one of God's perfections—God exists.

The Debate Resumed

"Hold on, there, please," says Immanuel Kant (1724–1804). "Existence is not a perfection. Existence is not a property of something, like its weight or its color might be. When we say the car is green, we are adding to its description. But we do not add to the *description* of a thing when we say that it exists. Rather, saying something exists is saying that something in reality corresponds to a certain description (that is, having such and such perfections). To assert existence is a different kind of activity than to list perfections. Second, existence is an all-or-nothing situation. There are no degrees of existence in the way there can be various weights or degrees of quality. For these two reasons, existence is not a perfection or attribute of anything, including God."

For Inquiry. What if Anselm were to reply, "That may be true of *contingent* things, those that can go in or out of existence. But it isn't true of *necessary* things, such as God. Existence is an essential element in the God concept. And it should have been included in the list in R-1! By definition, God exists, necessarily!"

Philosophical Role Playing

Defend the argument against Kant's objection. Argue the general case that given what God is, it is not possible that She or He should not exist.

R-5   THE PROBLEM OF EVIL

Question: Does God exist?

Challenge: If God is all-good and all-powerful, why is there evil?

A First Version of the Problem of Evil

God is omnipotent and benevolent. There is evil in the world. If benevolent, God would not have created evil. If omnipotent, God would have prevented evil. So, the God described above does not exist.

A Debate over the Argument

CRITIC: "But evil is an unreality. 'Evil' simply means the absence of good."

ADVOCATE: "You can't say that! Your definition of 'evil' doesn't fit with common usage. Saying that an action or event is evil is saying that, considered in itself, it would have been better had it never happened. Moral evil—like lying or murder—involves, or is the result of, human voluntary action. Natural evil—like a destructive earthquake or a crop-destroying storm—is evil that comes about in other ways, but not through human voluntary action. Evil is real."

CRITIC: "No, evil is an illusion of the human mind. It is just an emotional reaction to events that are otherwise without objective value."

ADVOCATE: "That won't work. First, evil is real. Second, if you say evil is an illusion, you will jeopardize the entire enterprise of connecting morality to religion. This does not fit with the view that God is the objective source of all value."

CRITIC: "Fine, so you want me to say that evil things really aren't so bad. They all serve good purposes."

ADVOCATE: "I would never say anything of the kind. A person who has lost a loved one to a tragic and unexpected accident would find either of the first two suggestions maliciously cruel. And saying evil isn't so bad would provide precious little solace. For even if good really did come from evil, then evil is certainly not unreal! And would it not have been a better world if evil were not required as a source of good? As Jesus' death on the cross and the Scriptural story of Job indicate, evil is both an emotional and rational challenge to religious faith."

CRITIC: "Just a minute. Your whole argument assumes that God had no compelling reason for allowing evil to exist. But there might be some excellent justifications for an all-loving and all-powerful God to create a world in which moral and natural evil would be possible. God created humans with free will so that they could choose to act in accordance with conscience and achieve virtue. But, in so doing, God recognized that moral evil would inevitably result. If humans were not free, then they would not really be persons. God decided that it is better to have persons in creation than to have a universe of mere animals, where neither sin nor salvation were possible."

ADVOCATE: "I'm familiar with that view—it is called the *free will justification*. Even if I were to agree, your objection explains moral evil, but it does not address why God permits natural evil."

CRITIC: "Yes, but the *soul-building justification* does. God wants humans to come to love and serve Him or Her freely. God knew the world was no Garden of Eden. But pain and suffering are not the worst things that can happen to humans. For, real as they are, they are also avenues through which salvation comes. Even the painful death of Jesus, evil as that event was, fits into God's plan as a redeeming source of great hope to all humankind. Both moral and natural evil have a place in God's plan. Human freedom is not an end in itself; it exists to help us come to serve and love God. With freedom comes both good and evil. Natural evil can be seen as divine retribution for sins or as a way for God to purify our faith and test the depth of our religious commitment, as in old man Job's case."

ADVOCATE: "Both approaches imply that God is responsible, at least indirectly, for moral evil. How can this be, if God is supremely ethical? Also, both approaches rely heavily on the concept of human freedom. But this concept is inconsistent with God's existence according to the arguments expressed in R-3. Finally, the soul-building justification leaves something out. What about the case of the good person who suffers deeply throughout life and never wavers in his or her religious commitment. Unless there is some final reward, the justification seems unfair. But this, in turn, suggests some kind of afterlife, at least for good people who suffer greatly and keep the faith. This involves us in all the metaphysical problems with life after death." (See N-1 through N-4.)

CRITIC: "I think too many unanswered questions remain for me to accept your argument as a valid demonstration that God cannot exist."

ADVOCATE: "In that case, let me modify it a little."

A Second Version of the Problem of Evil

Evil, both moral and natural, exists. If there was an intelligent designer of the universe, then one of two things is probably true: Either the designer was not motivated to do much about evil, or the designer was not capable of doing much about it. Thus, by analogy to human builders, God, the intelligent designer of the universe, was probably not all-powerful or not all-good.

Areas for Further Inquiry

The second version of the problem of evil inherits the objections raised against the design argument for God's existence regarding the weakness of analogical reasoning and the adequacy of the overall explanation. Looking at it this way, does God's existence or nonexistence change from being a matter of investigating a tentative empirical hypothesis to being a matter of attitudinal bias regarding how to interpret the human condition?

Philosophical Role Playing

Defend the view that evil is not the biggest threat to faith; comfort is a bigger challenge than adversity. The good life does not knock faith down; it erodes it. Religious commitment is tougher to maintain in times of softness, ease, and affluence than in times of trial and travail. Thus the tougher test is not the test of fire but the test of feathers.

R-6 THE COSMOLOGICAL ARGUMENT

Question: Does God exist?

Realization: Considering the universe as a totality, there must be some ultimate causal explanation for why something exists rather than nothing.

A Version of the Cosmological Argument

Each natural entity or event exists because of one or more causes. These causes can be other natural entities or events. Nothing can be the sole cause of its own existence. So, each natural entity or event in the world is caused, entirely or in part, by some other natural entity or event. Nothing can be the effect of an infinite causal chain. Therefore, there is a starting point in the causal chain called the universe, which is itself not a natural entity or event. This starting point, or first cause, we call God.

Is The First Cause Really God?

Does the *cosmological argument* accomplish its objective of proving God exists? A critic could take exception to the final statement saying, "Even if I agree a first cause exists, you still have not established that this first cause (1) still exists (2) is almighty, and (3) has the other attributes ordinarily associated with God."

St. Thomas Aquinas, a leading Catholic theologian of the thirteenth century and a philosopher whose work has influenced centuries of thinkers, realized these shortcomings. His "five ways" of proving God exists were intended to supplement each other by demonstrating different essential attributes of the divine. The five ways conclude that God is (1) the unmoved mover sustaining the motions of the planets and stars, (2) the first cause that led to the production of everything else, (3) the metaphysical source of all existence, (4) the qualitative standard against which we understand all perfection, and (5) the ultimate purpose giving direction and meaning to all creation.

Explaining Each and Explaining All

The guiding insight in the cosmological argument is comparable to that which governs something as elementary as the falling of dominoes. If they are all lined up, and the first one is tipped over, all will fall. To explain why any given one has fallen, you have two choices: (1) a *microexplanation*—this one fell because the one next to it fell and bumped it over; or (2) a *macroexplanation*—this one fell because it was one of a long series and something knocked over an earlier one in the series.

Philosophers who accept the first-cause argument assume that a macroexplanation is needed to make the universe understandable or intelligible. By contrast, science offers microexplanations. Science can help us understand the causal relationships between individual events, but science cannot explain why a universe exists in the first place. (See N-8 and L-5 on causality and scientific explanations.)

Areas for Further Inquiry

• Does the universe require an explanation? Why? Some philosophers, especially atheistic existentialists, maintain that we should simply accept absurdity as a fact of life.

• Even if a person accepts evolution and the big bang theory, even if that person agrees that there is no cosmic justice in the universe—no sense in which the good are rewarded and the evil are punished—and even if the person sees the universe as a constantly changing and self-generating reality, can that person avoid the question of why there is something rather than nothing without being intellectually dishonest?

R-7   FAITH AND REASON

Question: Is religious faith rational?

Analysis: A belief is rational if it is based on sufficient evidence and if the level of conviction is proportional to the quality of that evidence.

A Nonbeliever's Argument That Belief in God Is Irrational

NONBELIEVER: "If a belief is held in proportion to the evidence, then it is rational. The evidence for the proposition that God exists is weak, conflicting, and inconclusive. So, the belief that God exists is out of proportion to the evidence. Thus, that belief is not rational. To live the life of reason, one must act rationally. To act rationally, one should minimize one's chances of holding false beliefs. Therefore, one is acting irrationally if one believes in God."

A Debate over the Reasonableness of Belief in God

BELIEVER: "As it stands, your argument is not logical. A belief may be rational for other reasons than simply its proportionality to the evidence. I suggest you strengthen your first premise. One way would be to claim that *only* beliefs held in proportion to the evidence are rational."

NONBELIEVER: "It was kind of you to point that out. I agree and will substitute the stronger statement for my original one."

BELIEVER: "Well, I just didn't think it fair to criticize your position unless it was as solid as possible. In keeping with this, I must point out two more things. First, it is also irrational not to maximize one's chances of holding true beliefs. Your argument is too conservative. Life is full of risks and uncertainties. Second, I can't agree that the evidence for God's existence is as weak as you say."

NONBELIEVER: "Now I can't agree. The circumstances under which it is rational to maximize one's chance of holding true beliefs must be spelled out with care. Otherwise it is foolishness to accept statements as true without sufficient evidence only because you are trying to maximize your chance of being right. And as to the proofs for God's existence, none I've been shown are free of criticism. Even if one were, there would still be the problem of evil and the problem of free will to contend with." (See R-2 through R-6.)

BELIEVER: "We can reexamine the proofs later, but I want to focus on what you said about being rational. To always worry about avoiding error leads to intellectual paralysis, close-mindedness, prejudice, and lost opportunities. Nothing in this world is absolutely certain. You can't learn something unless you are willing to open your mind to new possibilities. Even at the risk of error, more is lost by suspending judgment than by actively pursuing the truth."

NONBELIEVER: "*Your* high-risk approach of believing out of proportion to the evidence can lead to close-mindedness, bias, and prejudice just as well as my conservative approach. In fact, what you want me to do is

146

worse—it's the essence of prejudice, namely believing something without having the evidence to back it up." (See T-1.)

BELIEVER: "Fine. Have it your way. Belief out of proportion to the evidence is irrational. But only *in some cases*. Belief in God *is an exception.*"

NONBELIEVER: "Don't lose your temper. I was criticizing your ideas, not you personally. Remember we are trying to have a sustained, philosophical discussion. All you have to do is give me *a reason* why an exception should be made in this case. Why is belief in God special?"

BELIEVER: "Forget it. What I want to say is that belief out of proportion to the evidence is rational *if the belief opens new opportunities to discovering the truth.* That is why belief in God is an exception."

NONBELIEVER: "Interesting. Which specific opportunities are lost or what kinds of new truths cannot be discovered if I decide not to risk believing in God?"

BELIEVER: "The risk is worth it because ultimately, without God, there are no objective values, and life is meaningless. That's why you should make your faith commitment. The act of faith gives direction and purpose to one's life. And that is precisely why it is rational to believe in God."

NONBELIEVER: "Hold on, I was talking about believing that God exists is a true statement. What you're talking about seems rather more dramatic."

BELIEVER: "You're right! And that's just it. There's a big difference between rational *thought* and rational *action*. A rational action takes into account the quality of the evidence, the importance of our goals, the urgency of the situation, the chances of success, and the relationship of what is risked to what might be gained. So, *the act of believing* in God might be rational, even if it is irrational to give *intellectual assent to the mere proposition* "God exists."

NONBELIEVER: "I accept the distinction. But, as William James (1842–1910) pointed out, there are criteria for deciding that an action is rational. To *act* out of proportion to the evidence one must be faced with a *momentous situation;* one must believe that the choice one is selecting to pursue is really a *live, not absurd or hopeless option;* and one must be *forced to act* rather than having the option of waiting. Do these three conditions fit in the case of believing in God?"

BELIEVER: "Yes! They do. Choosing *to live a life of religious faith* is precisely the kind of action that is a *live option* and a *serious one* as well. The choice is also *forced* because the practical consequences of suspending belief (agnosticism) and not believing (atheism) are identical. It may also have been James who pointed out that, in pragmatic terms, our only two choices are living out our belief in and commitment to God or living as an atheist."

147

NONBELIEVER: "You're shifting the discussion. Faith in God, meaning a personal commitment to God, is not the same as the intellectual belief in the truth of the proposition that God exists. Faith implies a personal relationship with the Almighty that operates on emotional and attitudinal levels in addition to the intellectual level. Belief is only intellectual. Our original discussion was about the *rationality of belief in the truth of the proposition that God exists*. Either you've missed the point, or your faith commitment is not based on reason."

BELIEVER: "But that *is* the point. There is a huge difference between belief in the truth of a proposition and the much fuller act of religious commitment to God. It's purely cerebral types such as you who are confused. The entire idea of trying to demonstrate the truth of the sterile statement 'God exists' fails to grasp the richness of a totally consuming religious faith. Faith in God's existence cannot be summed up in the insipid rationalizations of impotent intellectuals. Faith in God is a powerful, life-altering act involving the commitment of one's whole mind and spirit to the divine person. And it is not irrational!"

Areas of Further Inquiry

• Without God, can life have meaning and can values have objectivity? (See E-6.)

• Is religious faith in God rational or not? If it's irrational, does that imply it is, from philosophical and scientific perspectives, nonsense? Can something be irrational from one perspective and not from another? If so, what does this imply for the idea, presented in R-1, that truth is one?

• Most religions have propositional content such as that God approves of this, forbids that, intends this other thing, acts in such and such ways, and is characterized by thus and so attributes. How are honest intellectual disputes about a religion's propositional content to be rationally resolved?

THEORY

T-1   APPROACHES TO THEORY BUILDING

Question: How does one set about developing a philosophical theory?

Strategic observation: The best beginning might be in the middle.

Three Requirements

A general approach to theory building (or method of problem solving) should satisfy three criteria if we are to call it *rational*. First, it must tell us where we should begin attacking the problem. Second, it must suggest how to proceed toward a resolution. Third, it must tell us how to measure or evaluate our success.

The Foundationalist Approach

The more abstract *foundationalist* approach to building a philosophical position (theory, perspective) stresses (1) starting with *secure first principles* and (2) *being certain at each step along the way* not to let error have any chance to enter. For foundationalists, the goal is knowledge, understood as true justified belief.

In terms of the three requirements, *foundationalism* would propose that we, first, begin with those beliefs that we know beyond doubt to be absolutely certain. Second, we build on these indubitable first principles by adding those beliefs that the first principles suggest, at each step being sure our inferences rely only on arguments that are valid and sound (see L-3). Third, we measure our success by being able to give precise, error-free demonstrations regarding the certainty of everything we believe. (See K-1.)

The Contextualist Approach

The more pragmatic *contextualist* approach to building a philosophical perspective stresses (1) coming to a position that is as reasonable as possible given the subject matter being discussed and (2) being as fair as possible to the existing body of considered opinion regarding that subject. For contextualists, the goal is knowledge, understood as warranted assertability. (See K-1.)

In terms of the three requirements, contextualists would propose that we start by identifying a broad set of mutually agreed upon and well considered assumptions regarding whatever issue we are considering. Second, using sound arguments that can be either valid deductions or warranted inductions, we should build outward from this central set of assumptions toward a richer and fuller circle (or web) of beliefs. We may use any arguments in this process that are considered reasonable insofar as the subject matter being treated is concerned. Third, we should measure our success in terms of how comprehensive our beliefs are and how applicable they are to the original questions that motivated our inquiry.

Mutual Criticisms

The foundationalists object that the contextualists' approach has serious flaws. First, it cannot guarantee certainty because it starts with mutually agreed upon beliefs, of which one or more might be false. Second, even if the contextual approach starts out well enough, it allows error to enter along the way because it accepts the use of inductive reasoning (see L-5), where the premises give only probable support to their conclusions. Third, the contextualist approach does not measure up in terms of the philosophical goal of clarity and precision of thought (see P-2).

To these criticisms contextualists reply that the foundationalists are being unreasonable in their demands for certainty. The degree of assurance required to settle a given issue, say the contextualists, depends on the context in which the doubt arises and the degree of precision to which a given subject admits. You cannot, for example, reduce morality to mathematics!

Implicit in this reply is the contextualists' criticism of the foundationalists. First, the foundationalist program assumes that one can start fresh, believing nothing except what is certain and building from there. But in reality we do not, should not, and cannot start each inquiry without the benefit of any beliefs whatsoever. It is psychologically if not epistemologically impossible to carry out the foundationalists' program. Second, in being so concerned to avoid error, the foundationalists cut themselves off from an important source of truth, namely inductive inferences. Finally, the foundationalist approach sacrifices too much in its preoccupation with precision and clarity for it gives up on comprehensive systematicity and the evaluative purposes of philosophy (see P-2).

Areas for Further Inquiry

• In deciding which approach to favor, is it better to be ignorant but certain or correct but subject to doubt? Or, to put it another way, should one strive to believe as much truth as possible even if error creeps in or be conservative about what one believes, being sure always to avoid error? In what sense might the answer depend on the issue at hand?

• What would you think the foundationalists and the contextualists would say about the possibility of achieving *knowledge* in each of these subjects: physics, geometry, music, art, religion, ethics, metaphysics, formal logic, sociology, education, nursing, biology, marketing, politics, communications, computer science, and management science?

• Both the foundationalist and the contextualist approach would agree with the concept that proof must start someplace. Sooner or later, if you trace a person's proof for something back far enough, you will come to an initial primitive position from which the person has reasoned. At that point, the foundationalists would want to find certain and self-evident first principles, and the contextualists would hope to find a reasonable set of assumptions. In your considered opinion, who is looking for the right thing? Why do you think so?

T-2   EVALUATING THEORIES

Question: Given two theories, how can I tell which is better?

Insight: If we can say that science is better than superstition, then independent criteria for rationally judging the relative merits of competing theories must exist.

An Argument That Theories Cannot Be Evaluated

Theories are, by definition, abstract generalizations in contrast to specific observations of fact. "Truth" means correspondence to the facts of reality. Although two or more theoretical statements might be consistent, we cannot know whether or not they correspond to facts. So, we cannot know which theories are true. Therefore, there is no rational way to evaluate theories.

Possible Objections to the Argument

CRITIC: "First, the argument is self-defeating. The definition of 'truth' in the second statement is a theoretical definition. If we cannot evaluate theories, how can we know if that definition is adequate?" (See K-4.) "Second, and more seriously, the concept of a 'theory'—which your first statement assumes—is an incomplete concept. Theories are not just generalizations. Actually, theories are *conceptual systems*. As such, they include statements that serve at least four different kinds of functions:

1. Definitions of *primitive* terms. These definitions are used as conceptual starting points (e.g., line, atom, soluble, weight).

2. Definitions of *derived* terms. These assert conceptual connections be-tween primitive terms and other defined terms (e.g., circle, molecule).

3. *Assumptions.* These are lawlike statements taken as primitive truths. (e.g., through a point outside a line one and only one straight line can be drawn that is parallel to a given line).

4. *Theorems* are statements that can be inferred, inductively or deductively, on the basis of the other elements (e.g., sugar is soluble in water).

"Third, a conceptual system may yield theorems that admit of being tested by empirical methods. Thus, experience or observation can be very relevant to the evaluation of some theories. Be cautious, however, because some so-called facts exist only in the context of certain ways of defining words. That is, some predicate expressions are *theory laden* (e.g., . . . is a Freudian slip or . . . is a sinner)."

Four Criteria

Conceptual systems, or theories, can be compared to each other in terms of four important evaluative criteria.

1. *Comprehensiveness:* Given two theories, the one that accounts for the broadest spectrum of phenomena is considered superior. That is, the theory that is the more *complete* in terms of the kinds of issues addressed and explained is preferable compared to a theory narrow in scope. In philosophy, a theory that has metaphysical, epistemological, and norma-tive implications is superior to one that is restricted to resolving a single problem in only one of those broad areas.

2. *Consistency:* Given two theories, the one with the fewer internal in-consistencies or anomalies is superior. That is, the theory that is the more conceptually *coherent* is preferable as compared to a theory that must be frequently amended in order to deal with a purported coun-terexample or one that finds it necessary to redefine words in un-conventional and counterintuitive ways in order to circumvent self-contradiction.

3. *Simplicity:* Given two theories, the one with the fewest primitive terms and assumptions is considered superior. That is, the theory that is *logically* the least complex, in that it presupposes the fewest undefined or unobservable entities, is preferable compared to other theories that purport to account for the same phenomena but require acceptance of more assumptions and unobservables. (Notice that the issue here is relative structural simplicity, *not* psychological simplicty, which is how easy it might be to understand a theory.)

4. *Applicability:* Given two theories, the one that yields the more accurate predictions about phenomena is considered superior. That is, the theory that allows one to make more accurate observations, applications, and predictions about what will occur under such and such conditions is preferable compared to a theory that yields either no predictions or unreliable predictions. Theories, even philosophical ones, that are tied to experience and help us make sense out of the human condition are superior to those that are idle, speculative fantasies.

Areas for Further Inquiry

• As suggested in T-1, comprehensiveness puts stress on consistency. Similarly, applicability often requires greater logical complexity. If decisions must be made between the realization of each of these virtues, which should be compromised and how far?

• How do the four criteria relate to the evaluative considerations used to assess models and analogies? (See L-4.)

Philosophical Role Playing

In M-4 there is a discussion of *internal* and *external* criticisms of *normative theories*. Generalize that discussion to apply to the evaluation of all kinds of theories (e.g., scientific theories or theories of government or theories of human nature). Explain how internal and external kinds of criticisms relate to the criteria of consistency, applicability, and comprehensiveness.

T-3   COUNTEREXAMPLES AND WORLD VIEWS

Question: Do I have a world view; if so, what is it?

Insight: Human knowledge can never be complete. What one knows and can know depends on one's education, historical setting, insight, and world view.

Counterexamples and Where They Lead

The practice of presenting an opinion so that others might examine it and offer counterexamples is instructive for what it reveals about both how intellectual progress occurs and how we, as complex persons, operate. Suppose philosopher A proposes a theory of human nature (see N-6 for examples). Philosopher A says human nature can be defined as X, Y, and Z. At some point, philosopher B presents counterexamples, which B claims show either that the theory is too strong (X, Y, and Z exclude some cases that should not be excluded) or too weak (some cases that should be excluded happen to satisfy X, Y, and Z). At this point the debate has begun—not ended—regarding the adequacy of the theory A is trying to present. These kinds of transactions represent only the *first of four* levels or kinds of interactions regarding the theory.

At the *second* level A responds to the critic, B. The responses involve amending and improving the original theory in order to take into account the kinds of counterexamples presented. This can be considered a normal and necessary part of refining one's point of view. Or a more negative interpretation can be put on it. The amendments might be narrowly ad hoc, meaning they serve no theoretical purpose except to rule out specific counterexamples. The difference between an "acceptable amendment" and an "unacceptably ad hoc quick fix" is largely psychological. Ideally, however, worthy amendments are aimed at addressing *kinds* of problems, not simply this or that specific odd or anomalous case.

At the *third* level, after the give and take of counterexample and amendment has run its course, B tries to mount an attack on the fundamental assumptions undergirding A's theory. Critic B tries to show that *the reason* the theory requires continuous repair is that it is misguided in some important and fundamental way. It could happen that at this level of the debate, while A and B have locked horns, someone else, C, suggests a new, innovative proposal for how to reconceive and resolve the original issue.

Some debates reach a *fourth* level; at this level it is clear that A's and B's basic intuitions have come into conflict. If the third level yielded no satisfactory solution—perhaps because A's defense was sturdy, B's case was not persuasive, or no new innovative approach to the problem emerged—then the discussion, if it continues at all, returns to the counterexamples. This time they are scrutinized in detail as A and B debate whether they are "genuine" or not. What emerges as the key issue at the fourth level is the comparative adequacy of the different understandings A and B have of the concept originally being analyzed or the question originally discussed. They might learn that they are concerned with, talking about, and trying to understand similar, but still slightly different, things. Often only an analysis of such borderline cases as those suggested as counterexamples can reveal these subtle but crucial differences. And this realization, too, is progress.

World Views

The jump from theories to world views is not one of kind but of scope and impact. World views are conceptual systems (see T-2), like theories, but much more intellectually complete and psychologically forceful. A world view is a broadly systematic overview of fundamental human questions, categories of thoughts, and life concerns.

Fully developed world views provide one with insights and "answers" to questions and concerns in *metaphysics, epistemology,* and *value theory.* Among other things, a world view defines what reality is, how we can know reality, and what, if any, normative inferences we can draw regarding any aspect of reality. Questions regarding God's existence, human freedom, human nature, personal identity, personal morality, social responsibility, the acquisition of truth, the appreciation of beauty, and the meaning of life are addressed by any comprehensive world view, whether that world view be derived from sources that are religious, philosophical, empirical, social, or cultural.

World views can collide. In one's effort to understand reality and the human condition, one often encounters the clashing perspectives of hostile world views. (For example: Was the world created or did it evolve? Is a fetus a person with moral rights, or is the abortion issue a matter of individual freedom and autonomy? Should the state have the right to mislead or manipulate people for its own noble, long-term purposes, or do individual rights take priority? Should one strive for knowledge by seeking certainty through avoiding error or by opening the mind to broader, but less certain, possibilities? Are the microexplanations of science the only legitimate kinds of explanations, or should one consider certain macroexplanations?)

When world views conflict, what should we do? The rational approach to this problem—provided it is not rationality itself that is at stake—is to use the four criteria in T-2 to evaluate the adequacy of competing systems of thought. But it would be naive to think that the evaluation will be exclusively rational and not in part psychological or emotional.

Areas for Further Inquiry

In day-to-day conversations with others who share one's world view, the inadequacies of that world view are seldom noticed. But on occasion one is drawn out of one's intellectual comfort zone and confronted with challenges, both rational and emotional, to the adequacy of one's world view. When that happens, the potential for a *personal conceptual revolution* emerges. People have experienced radical shifts in their world views. Depending on one's perspective, such a person might be said to have been "brainwashed" or "converted." Such a dramatic change in world view is not the neutral discovery of new facts. It is more the mind-jolting feeling that *the entire universe has changed.*

Although the universe itself remains exactly as it was, a person might

155

describe her or his experience this way: "Where once I thought of myself as alone, a trivial biological happenstance on a piece of cosmic dust spinning through the cold void of space, I now realize I am a child of the Almighty, alive and loved by the One who constantly watches over me." A similar "Eureka!" experience can occur not just in the realm of religion, but in one's *view* of scientific "reality" or political "reality" or interpersonal "reality."

The question is, should opportunities for personal conceptual revolutions be sought or be avoided? To philosophize or not philosophize, that is the question!

INDEX